Rosemary Hauck McCandless

Stefanie Rae Smith

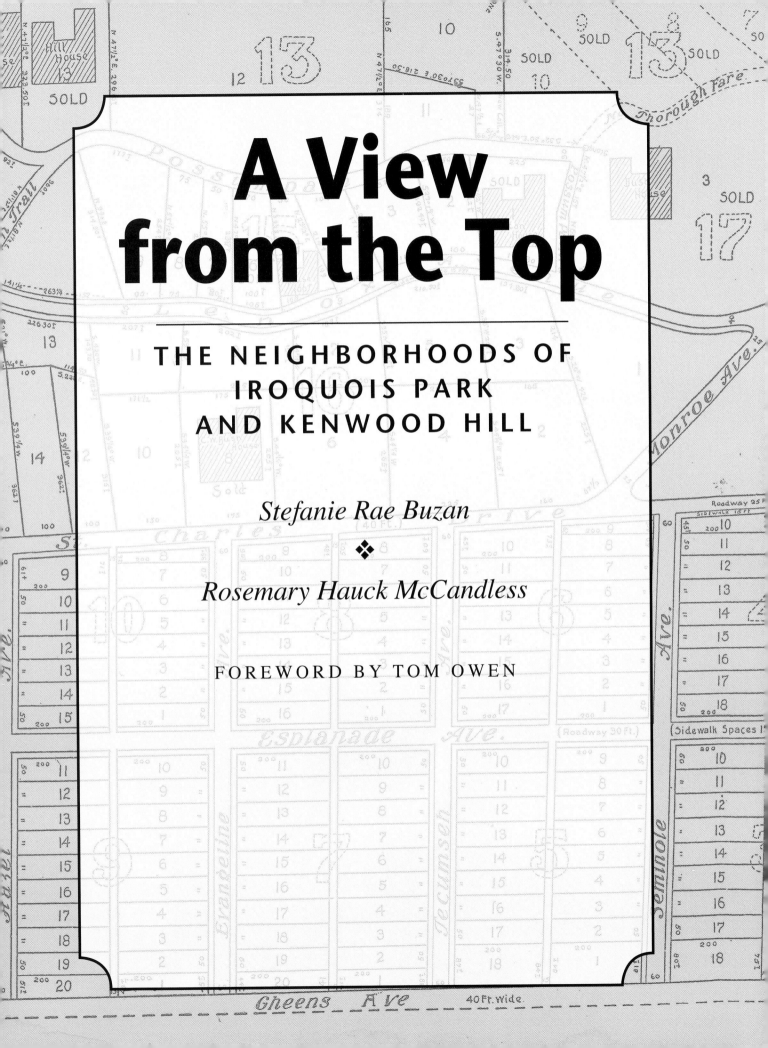

A View from the Top

THE NEIGHBORHOODS OF IROQUOIS PARK AND KENWOOD HILL

Stefanie Rae Buzan

❖

Rosemary Hauck McCandless

FOREWORD BY TOM OWEN

Table of Contents

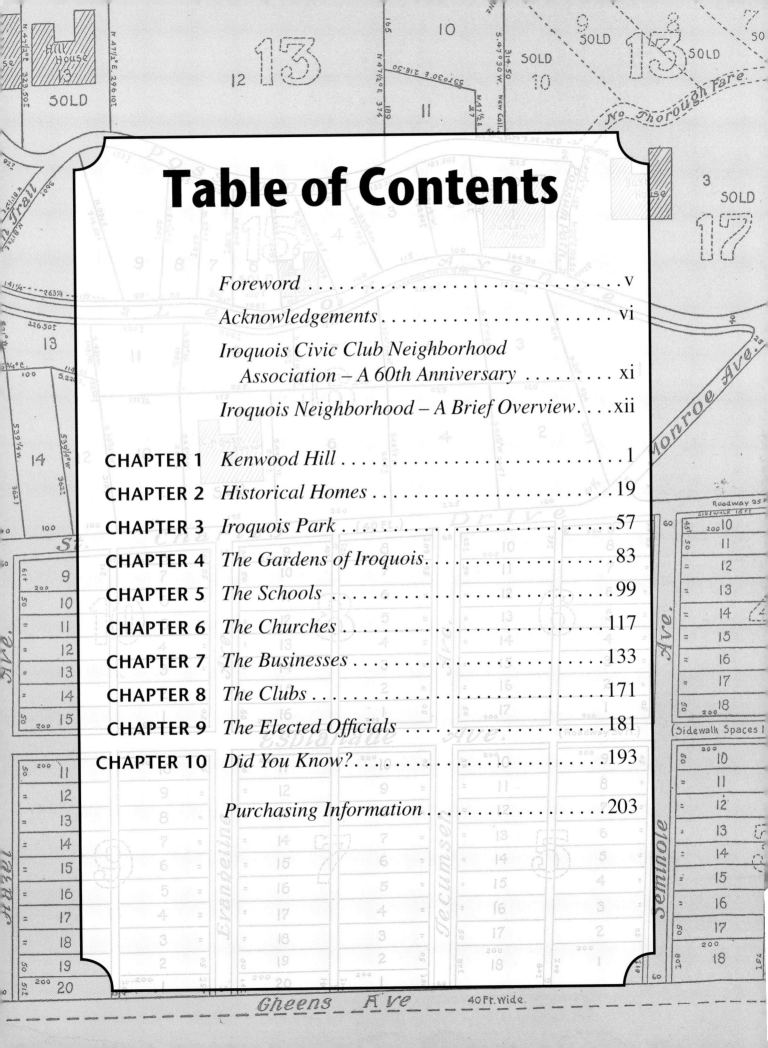

Foreword

Place and time have been intertwined since humans had breath. In Bible times, places frequently got their names because of some storied event that had happened there. The mere calling of the place-name evoked the lively re-telling of a pivotal happening where the Divine and Humankind met. In this sense, Faulkner correctly observed that "The Past is Never Dead. It is not even the Past."

A View from the Top is a celebration of the Iroquois neighborhood's past. Earlier actors in the saga of that place come to life here and leave their names on modern-day intersections, street-names, hillside retreats, old playgrounds, and grand homes. But there is much more involved here than simply what happened long ago. The production of this book, for instance, is testimony to the tireless, collective energies of neighborhood researchers and compilers who delight in the Iroquois story and believe its telling builds pride in place for today's residents and deepens appreciation for the old neighborhood for those who used to call it "home". Finally, books have a way of enduring and future generations of Southenders should see this good work as a baton of hope and aspiration for the old neighborhood passed to them by folks who deeply believe in the collective power of well-intentioned community.

Place and time are richly blended in the story and photos contained in A View from the Top. Indeed, for those who love the Southend, a stroll through these pages will evoke a Past that in many ways ". . . is not even the Past."

Tom Owen
University of Louisville
September, 2006

We would like to thank all the people who made this book possible. Many people opened their homes to us or shared their time over the phone to tell us the stories that are in this book. They dug through their attics, closets, cedar chests, or mom's attics, closets and cedar chests, to find old photos and various documents to add to the stories. We were amazed at their generosity. This book was started hoping to tell some of the wonderful stories we had heard and each story led to more people and more stories. It is truly amazing how inter-connected we all are in this area. We learned so much about the rich history of this area from all of you who shared with us and hope the readers will also enjoy "the view from the top".

INTERVIEWS

Charles (Bud) Farmer
Bill Tafel Sr.*
Lorretta Walker*
Jane Charmoli *
Susan Harris Wilburn*
Linda Savage
Patty and Fred Banks
Jim Fitzgibbon*
Lillian Preston Perkins*
Sonja Gordon
Margie Simms Gibson*
Michael Siegel
Steve Phelps
Betty Scott*
Johnnie Gordon Royalty
Ted and Regina Zirnheld*
Ethel and Jack Glass*
John Bryant
Caroline Drexler Hollis*
Helen Yates
Al Stogner
Bill and Nell King*
Swag Hartel
Irma Atwell*
Lonnie Ray
William Senning Jr. *
George Ray *
Russell "Bud" Puckett
James Thornberry

Helen and David Cecil*
Ray Cooper*
Marshall Morrison
Brad Wilson
George (Buz) Bush*
Sharon Seum
George and Janet Pierson*
Dr. Mark Brockman
Gloria Brockman Montgomery*
Dr. John Larson Jr.
Mary Ellen Rateau Clements*
Bertha Goss
Dr. and Mrs. Irvin Bronner*
Captain Alan Boucher (Kenwood Fire Station)
David Cecil
Bob Burge
Bob Coke*
Bob West
Rich Schulten
Dick Cooper
M.E. (Red) Smith
Thelma Carter*
Herb and Linda Philips*
Sandy Bush Supinger*
Al Boesmer*
Arthur Hendricks*
Mary Ann Gocke
Joyce Peck*
Edith Hatfield

And all the others who gave us names of people to contact. We apologize if we left anyone out.

* Also gave photographs and/or documents

PHOTOGRAPHS and/or DOCUMENTS

Amy Decker, (St. Mark Lutheran Church)
Pastor Michelle Elfers, (St. Mark Lutheran Church)
Etta Cook and Steve Jeffries, (Historians Epiphany Methodist Church)
Josh Blandford, (DeSales High School)
Pastor David Blair, (Epiphany Methodist Church)
Ethel Gardner, (Epiphany Methodist Church)
Steve Sims, (Auburndale Baptist Church)
Pastor Brian Croft, (Auburndale Baptist Church)
Reverend Dale Cieslik (Archdiocesan Archives)
Dave and Mary Winges
Randy Beard, (Senior Minister Kenwood Heights Christian Church)
Rev. Phillip L. Erickson (St. Thomas More Catholic Church)
Rebecca Maddox (Southwest Branch Public Library)
Tom Owen (U of L Archives)
Sally Moss (Little Loomhouse)
Cecilia May (Our Lady of Mount Carmel)
Charlie Atchinson (Naval Ordnance)
Bill King (Naval Ordnance)
Joe Willen (Naval Ordnance)
Pastor Donnie Gullion (Lynn Acres Baptist Church)
Michael Steinmacher (Beechmont Public Library)
Mary Margaret Bell (Jefferson Co. Public Schools)
Carolyn S. Smither (Olmsted Conservancy)
Alan Nations (Olmsted Conservancy)
Daryl Hamrick (James W. Sewall Co.)
Bill Kubota (KDN Films)
Ruth Compton (Rutherford Elementary)
Paula Weglarz (The Berry Mansion)
Barbara Terranova (Little Loomhouse)
Benida Crask (St. Thomas More)
Rusty Cummings (Auburndale Auto Parts)
Pete Gibson
Bobby Escher
John Story
Lee Ebner
Kitty Tenny
Beverly Wheatley
Morton Childress
The Rice Family
The Berry Mansion
William Hendricks
Ann Underbrink
Kathy Bronner
Greg Kastan
Barbara Nichols

*Photograph of Bill Cecil arriving home on Southside Drive
from Auburndale School is courtesy of the Cecil Family.
Kenwood Drive-In is in the background.*

SOURCES

Lyons Papers, U of L Archives
      Lillian Preston Perkins
      Janice Johnson
Personal interviews
Ancestry.com
DriveIns.com
City Directories
The Filson Club
The Berry Mansion
Archdiocese of Louisville Archives
The Southern Magazine 1894
Library Files (downtown branch)
U of L Photographic Archives
U of L Archives, neighborhood files
Courier-Journal and Louisville Times
Louisville City Records, deeds and wills
Jefferson County Public Schools Archives
Louisville Bicycle Club website - Joe Ward
History of Louisville, Vol.2, 1897
      Chapter 34, The Public Parks and Parkways, by Andrew Cowan
Individual Church Histories provided by the churches
Louisville Landmarks (Richard Jett)
The Little Loomhouse A Brief History by Alice Davidson
WJ Dodd Website (Christopher White)
DeSales Freshman Year Book 1956
The Gheens Foundation
      A Story of Stewardship
      The Life and Legacy of Mr. and Mrs. Charles Edwin Gheens

Photograph of Florence Rateau Thomas, Mary Ellen Rateau Clements and Thelma Crum dancing on Fay Avenue, circa the early 1940s, is courtesy of Mary Ellen Rateau Clements.

RESEARCHERS

Stefanie Rae Buzan
Tony Buzan
Rosemary Hauck McCandless
Garry W. McCandless, Sr.
Robin Amsbary
David Winges
Mary Winges
Diane Hoagland
Beverley Wheatley
Sally Moss
Barbara Nichols
Lillian Preston Perkins
Paula Weglarz

Photograph of the 1936 Eighth Grade class of Auburndale School is courtesy of Lillian Preston Perkins.

WRITERS

Stefanie Rae Buzan
Rosemary Hauck McCandless

CONTRIBUTING WRITERS

Diane Hoagland
Robin Amsbary
Susan Harris Wilburn
David C. Fowler
Dave Winges
Alan Nations
Alice Davidson

Margaret Merrick
Fred Banks
Thelma Carter
Dolores Delahanty
William Hendricks
Joan Sternberg Butler

EDITORS

Tony Buzan
Garry W. McCandless, Sr.

Annie Mattingly
Barbara Hauck Binder

DESIGN AND PRODUCTION

Kate Binder/Prospect Hill Publishing Services • Beechmont Press

Photograph of New Cut Road, facing north, Colonial Gardens is on the right, Iroquois Park is on the left, is used with the permission of the University of Louisville Photographic Archives.

We would like to thank those who helped turn the dream of this book into a reality.

Dan Johnson, District 21 Councilman
Republic Bank
Iroquois Area Business Association
National City Bank
Dr. and Mrs. Irvin E. Bronner
Marianthe and Tom Masterson

2006 Artist sketch of Mayor Charles Jacob
by Tony Buzan

We would like to give special thanks to Barbara Nichols, President of the Iroquois Neighborhood Association and Civic Club who supported the development of this book from the first discussions through the publication, believing in the project and giving help and guidance all along the way.

The Iroquois Civic Club Neighborhood Association
A 60th Anniversary

As one of Louisville's oldest neighborhood associations, the Iroquois Neighborhood Association has been a vital source of positive change. Throughout its sixty years of activity, the Iroquois Neighborhood Association has worked as an advocate for

Louisville's South End. Neighborhood improvements have included expanded sewer systems, road construction, beautification projects and a petition to downzone portions of the neighborhood from R5 to R4 in an effort to protect the area's green space and the structural integrity of the homes. The efforts to improve the quality of life for people in the South End continue, and the Iroquois Neighborhood Association invites you to join with them in this endeavor.

Photographs of the flag dedication at Iroquois Park are courtesy of Barbara Nichols, President of the Iroquois Neighborhood Association and Civic Club.

Iroquois Neighborhood A Brief Overview
Contributed by Margaret Merrick

The swampy wetlands and salt ponds of the Ohio Valley became hospitable sources of food for large herds of grazing buffalo following migratory runs through what was to become Jefferson County. Cherokee Indians, who also roamed the area, laid in wait for the buffalo that ventured between the promontories known as Sunshine Hill (Kenwood) and Burnt Knob (Iroquois). They made their camp and dried their animal hides on the limestone outcropping of the Devil's Backbone on Sunshine Hill.

Louisville was incorporated as a city in 1780. As settlements along the banks of the Ohio gained importance in the westward push, large tracts of land surrounding this busy river town were deeded to prominent families who started residential and commercial developments in the area.

Between 1784 and 1840, the Phillips family acquired 1,200 acres of land seven miles south of the river. This tract included two largely wooded hills and surrounding slopes. In 1864, Benoni Figg purchased most of Sunshine Hill (Kenwood), at this time referred to as Cox's Knob, from the Phillip's family. Figg operated a lumber mill and a charcoal operation on this newly acquired property. In time, Figg replaced much of the Old Central Plank Road (now known as Third Street), a corduroy road of logs, with stone from his quarry on Cox's Knob. He also laid out Strawberry Lane leading to the Strawberry Station on the L & N line. In 1876, Figg sold 126 acres of the north slope of Cox's Knob to his son-in-law, Charles Gheens.

The 1890s were a period of land speculation and building. The St. James area off Fourth Street was redeveloped from a farm exhibition arena to stately homes and an adjacent park. Further south, plans were laid for the Meadow Brook development between Kenwood Way and Kingston Avenue. At this time Charles Gheens sold much of his land holdings in the Iroquois area to Sam Stone Bush and the Kenwood Park Residence Company. At the same time, City of Louisville Mayor Charles Jacob bought 300 acres of Burnt Knob for the city's largest park, first known as Jacob's Park. The Fourth Street streetcar line was extended past Churchill Downs, down Third Street to the entrance of this new city park. By 1897, Senning's Park was an established entertainment center at the corner of Kenwood Avenue and New Cut Road. During the early Twentieth Century, development in the Iroquois area was primarily confined to summer retreats with a few select homes built around the wooded slopes of the two hills.

Development in the Iroquois area began again at the end of the 1930s when Kenwood Park Residence Company sold building sites in an area aptly named Kenwood Village and Southlawn. The Iroquois Amphitheater was built by Works Progress Administration. Iroquois Garden, just south of the park, held a grand opening with Mike Riley's Orchestra. In 1939, Lou Tate bought property on Kenwood Hill that sheltered three summer homes of the Bush family and a wagon shed left by Benoni Figg. This property was to become a gathering place for textile artists and crafts persons and became known as the Little Loomhouse.

The 1940s and World War II brought dramatic changes to the Iroquois area. In 1940, the U. S. Navy selected Louisville as the location for a naval ordnance factory. By October 1941, this station was preparing to open with a projected workforce of 1,700 workers. Local industries lent personnel and area schools trained machinists and factory workers to provide a workforce for the defense plant. Although the numbers of workers fluctuated throughout the years, at one-time, the Naval Ordnance Station was the fourth largest industrial employer in the Louisville area.

Housing development in the South End was greatly impacted by the growth of the Naval Ordnance Station. Land surrounding the plant was developed in order to build 150 low cost two and three bedroom homes for the defense workers.

Photograph of the construction of St. Thomas More Catholic Church and School and the surrounding neighborhood located at 3ʳᵈ and Inverness is courtesy of St. Thomas More Catholic Church.

In the throes of post war prosperity, development of the Iroquois area began in earnest. In 1947, LeRoy Highbaugh laid out the Lynn Acres subdivision between Southside Drive and Louisville Avenue. The same year, Southland Park Subdivision bounded by Steedly Avenue, Southside Drive and Strawberry Lane was built. Kenwood Heights, Iroquois View and Kenwood Manor subdivisions were built on the north and west slopes of Kenwood Hill. T.G. Eckles and his son, William Eckles, built 400

Photograph of the former home of LeRoy Highbaugh, at 1032 Runell Road, March 2006, is courtesy of Stefanie Buzan.

homes in Kenwood Heights and Iroquois Acres. In the 1960s, the Eckles began developing Kenwood Estates toward the summit of Kenwood Hill while Robert Thieneman was developing Kenwood Terrace on the southern slopes of Iroquois Hill. By the end of the 1960s the residential character of the Iroquois area was well established.

Just as the secluded summer homes designed to shelter people from the heat of the city attracted people to the Iroquois area, the post war development provided people with homes in this attractive area. With the advent of these developments came improved roads, sewer lines, schools, churches, businesses and recreational facilities. This growth fostered community spirit, which in turn, encouraged citizen input and service. The Iroquois Neighborhood Association has for sixty years encouraged its citizens to continue this spirit and service to the community.

The Rateau Family, circa the late 1920s, on the front porch of their home on Fay Avenue.
Kenwood Drive and Kenwood Hill are in the background. The photograph is courtesy of
Mary Ellen Rateau Clements.
Back row: Dad (Clarence), Grandpa Rateau (Leopold)
Front row: Charles, Mary Ellen, Mom (Margaurite), Earl and Florence

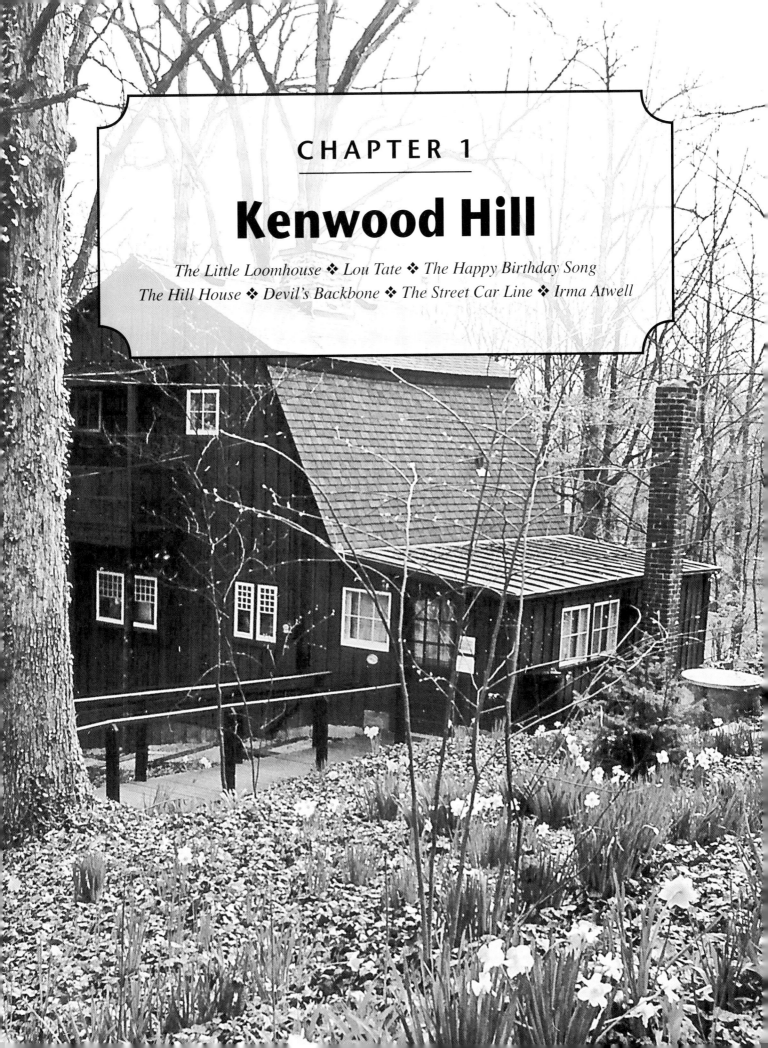

CHAPTER 1

Kenwood Hill

The Little Loomhouse ❖ *Lou Tate* ❖ *The Happy Birthday Song*
The Hill House ❖ *Devil's Backbone* ❖ *The Street Car Line* ❖ *Irma Atwell*

The Chronological History of the Little Loomhouse
Home of Lou Tate
328 Kenwood Hill Road

During an architectural convention in Louisville, KY, Frank Lloyd Wright stole away in order to visit the Little Loomhouse. His observation prompted him to describe the Victorian summer homes in these words, "Three board and batten cabins set in the dignity of nature under the mighty oaks of Kenwood Hill" This observation holds true in 2006. The next couple of pages will take you on a journey of the rich history of the unique place called the Little Loomhouse.

1860s (Late) Benoni Figg acquired a tract of land from the Phillips family. Benoni Figg had a charcoal business and started a limestone quarry on Kenwood Hill. He built a cabin (known today as Esta) as an office, as well as quarters for his caretakers. The cabin originally consisted of just two rooms with vertical split log siding. According to one of Figg's daughters, the outside wooden stairway leading to the second story was built to prevent the caretaker from entering the business office.

1876 Due to business reverses, the cabin was sold to Charles W. Gheens, the husband of Figg's daughter, Mary. It was converted to a summer home for his family.

1890s (Late) Sam Stone Bush, Secretary of the Kenwood Residential Company, acquired the cabin from the Gheens family and remodeled it again. During one of these remodelings the siding was changed to the board and batten style. Bush also built the other two cabins Wisteria and Tophouse. All three cabins were used for summer homes. Bush would go on to develop the trolley system that connected Louisville's South End with the Downtown area.

1898 Etta Hast, an artist, purchased Esta and originated the tradition of it as a center for cultural life in Southern Jefferson County. She established an annual Strawberry Festival for artists, writers and teachers. The Hill sisters, noted kindergarten and music teachers who had a summer cabin up Kenwood Hill, wrote the Happy Birthday song which was first sung in Esta.

Photograph of the Little Loomhouse Cabins from bottom to top, Esta, Wisteria and Top House, winter 2004, is courtesy of Stefanie Buzan.

1907 Mary Wulff, a writer and artist, bought the cabin complex and continued using them for community oriented events. An early Sunday school class held in Esta led to the founding of St. Mark Lutheran Church on Southside Drive. Mrs. Wulff held special gatherings to which she invited Kentucky artists, poets, and writers, as well as neighboring residents who had built summer log cabins on the hillside. She always included children in these parties. Lou Tate once said her first acquaintance with Esta was during such a visit. It was during Mrs. Wulff's time that the cabin was named Esta, which is said to be an old Norse saying meaning, "May God's presence be in this dwelling." The name still is visible on the cabin's door.

Author Mary Virginia Wulff at Esta Cabin circa 1924.

1934 Eleanor Roosevelt commissioned Lou Tate to weave linens for the White House while her husband was in office. On White House letterhead, Eleanor Roosevelt wrote the following: "What would you charge to make a luncheon set consisting of a runner for the middle of the table and twelve mats and twelve napkins, with just a little "R" woven on them in white".

Photograph of Lou Tate displaying her linen work is courtesy of the Little Loomhouse.

1935 Eleanor Roosevelt paid Lou Tate $16.75 for one luncheon set in white with an "R" in the center.

Historic documents: correspondence from Eleanor Roosevelt and copy of check she used for payment are courtesy of the Little Loomhouse.

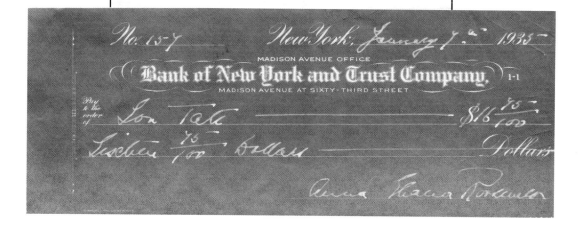

1938 Lou Tate's mother purchased the cabin complex and property from Mary Wulff's estate as a retirement home and space for Tate's weaving business. Sadly, Lou Tate's mother died shortly thereafter. Tate inherited the property and lived and worked there for the rest of her life. She utilized the cabins as a gathering place for weavers and those interested in learning to weave.

Eleanor Roosevelt paid a visit. As she entered Esta her foot went through a loose board. After noticing a number of other boards, which had been initialed, she asked for paint and a brush and added her name. This bit of history has long ago disappeared.

1939 Lou Tate begins a fellowship program to teach weaving to students at the Little Loomhouse. The students were sponsored by Eleanor Roosevelt.

Lou Tate started an experimental weaving group, The Kentucky Weavers Guild, and started publishing the Kentucky Weaver Magazine. She also began collecting contemporary hand-woven textiles in addition to her collection of traditional woven coverlets, which were exhibited both nationally and internationally.

1944 Lou Tate began working with Eleanor Roosevelt and the American Red Cross to incorporate Lou Tate's Little Loom as part of a rehabilitation program for hospitalized servicemen and women.

1970s Spinning was added to the teaching curriculum at the Little Loomhouse. Lou Tate used the cabins for many open houses, as well as formal classes and workshops. She also taught college extension courses in the greater Louisville area and surrounding states and did research on early American coverlets for universities.

Mark and Bruce Winges, circa the 1960s, practice their weaving techniques on one of Lou Tate's famous Little Looms at a spring open house. Photograph is courtesy of Dave and Mary Winges.

Today, Esta Cabin is used to illustrate some of the Little Loomhouse history. The first floor has a historic display featuring the life and career of Lou Tate as well as examples of weaving and spinning artifacts and equipment.

The upstairs area contains Lou Tate's numbered patterns and weaving information. There are organized files with photos and letters written by Lou Tate, as well as the archives of The Lou Tate Foundation from its beginning in 1979.

Wisteria serves as the Foundation Office, with an expanded Gift Shop. The original kitchen has been removed and its space holds extra weaving equipment and supplies. The extensive collection of weaving and related periodicals has found a new home on shelves surrounding the fire place in the office area.

Tophouse remains the studio for most of the weaving activities. Its years of service to the cause of keeping hand-weaving alive are a reason for pride. The Little Loomhouse cabins continue to delight school children, college students, tourists from all over the world, social groups, teachers, researchers and writers.

In 2005, Tom Whitus, Silver Hills Pictures and KDM used the Little Loomhouse as the setting for a full length horror film, The Devoured. The film was shot in 18 days and had a total budget of $300,000. Esta was the primary location for the filming of the movie while the Loomhouse staff conducted business as usual in Tophouse and Wisteria. The film is just the latest addition of artistic flair to the already colorful history of the cabins.

Interior of Esta Cabin 2005. Above is a reproduction of an original bench that once sat in Esta Cabin. The reproduction was hand crafted by Orville Moss. A vintage coverlet, 49 Snowballs, is draped over the back of the bench. Left: the original fireplace made from stone quarried on Kenwood Hill. Photographs are courtesy of Stefanie Buzan.

Lou Tate Bousman 1906-1979
Contributed by Alice Davidson

Lou Tate Bousman, known professionally as Lou Tate, was born in Bowling Green, Kentucky on October 19, 1906. Her ancestors were settlers in Virginia as early as 1790. Her father, J. H. Bousman, migrated as a young man to Kentucky where he became a conductor on the old L&N Railroad. In 1920, he was transferred to Louisville and the family bought a house at 1725 South Third Street.

Lou Tate graduated from the Louisville Girls High School in 1924. She spent one year at the University of Louisville before enrolling at Berea College where she earned a B.A. degree, followed by a Master of Arts in History from the University of Michigan.

Her interest in weaving began when she received five generations of weaving patterns from an elderly weaver, Miss Nan Owen. From then on she began her unique contribution as an American hand-weaving historian. Collecting old patterns, called drafts, took her into the far reaches of Kentucky – often on horseback. Her first local exhibitions of Kentucky hand weavings were held at the J. B Speed Museum in Louisville in 1937.

During the depression, she worked at President Hoover's Dark Hollow School for mountain children deep in the Blue Ridge Mountains of Virginia. Her contacts with Mrs. Hoover led to the development of the Lou Tate Table Loom (the Little Loom), first constructed by Dr. S. W. Mather, a Louisville dentist. Mrs. Hoover had approached Tate for a weaving project suitable for girl scouts, one of Mrs. Hoover's main interests. Her Little Loom was sold for over 20 years, both in this country and abroad. Many of her looms are still in use today.

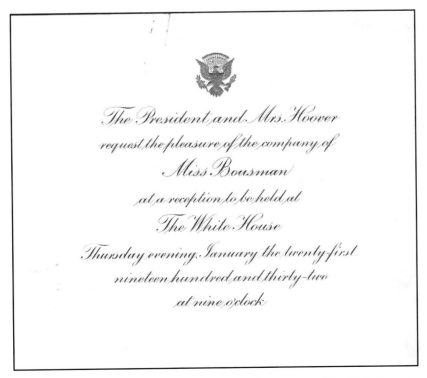

Historic document: Invitation to the White House is courtesy of the Little Loomhouse.

Later, Tate and her loom were given national exposure in Eleanor Roosevelt's syndicated column, My Day. In the early 1940s, Mrs. Roosevelt paid a visit to the Little Loomhouse and ordered a woven luncheon set for the White House.

In the 1940s, Tate started an experimental weaving group, The Kentucky Weavers Guild, and started publishing the Kentucky Weaver Magazine. She also began collecting contemporary hand-woven textiles in addition to her collection of traditional woven coverlets, which were exhibited both nationally and internationally. Tate's custom weaving business soon gave way to her first love, teaching—particularly introducing young children to this ancient form of folk art. Her own methods of teaching very young children also stimulated interest in history. During World War II, Tate extended her weaving skills to helping the hospitalized soldiers as a good form of physical therapy. She published several booklets and magazine articles on Kentucky weaving history, early coverlet patterns, and weaving techniques.

Spinning was added in the 1970s. She used the cabins for many open houses, as well as formal classes and workshops. She also taught college extension courses in the greater Louisville area and surrounding states. Unfortunately, illnesses and lack of resources to maintain the cabins plagued the last few years of her life. However, her contributions to the revival of hand-weaving in Kentucky, the preservation of old coverlets and their patterns, and encouragement of the contemporary experimental weaving were a true legacy in this field of folk art.

Lou Tate and Eleanor Roosevelt examine Blooming Leaf coverlets.
Photograph courtesy of the Courier-Journal.

The Little Loomhouse and the Happy Birthday Song

The Little Loomhouse complex is a location that has seen a lot of history. A significant part of the Loomhouse history is the first singing of the *Happy Birthday* song, one of the most popular songs in the English language.

Esta, which means, "May God's presence be in this dwelling" is the earliest of the three cabins in the Little Loomhouse complex. Esta was first built as an office for a rock quarry located on Kenwood Hill in Louisville, Kentucky and was later converted into a summer home for residents of Downtown Louisville to use as an escape from the heat. Esta's popularity sparked the construction of two additional summer homes, built in a cabin style, on the same site. The two new additions were named Wisteria and Tophouse.

In 1898, Etta Hast, an artist, purchased the cabin and originated the tradition of its use as a center for cultural life in southern Jefferson County. She established an annual Strawberry Festival for artists, writers and teachers. The Hill sisters, Mildred and Patty, noted kindergarten and music teachers, also authors of the Song Stories for the Kindergarten, owned the neighboring summer cabin just up the hill on Possum's Path.

During a birthday party given for Etta's sister, Lisette, neighbor, Patty Hill changed the words to one of the Hill sisters' songs from *Good Morning to All* to *Happy Birthday to You,* to mark the occasion, thus, the lyrics for *Happy Birthday* originated at Esta cabin on Kenwood Hill. Unbeknownst to anyone in attendance, the song would go on to become one of the most popular songs ever written.

Although the original music and lyrics, *Good Morning to All,* had been copyrighted, the "new" lyrics were not copyrighted until 1935, which meant under federal law the copyright would not expire until 75 years later—the year 2010.

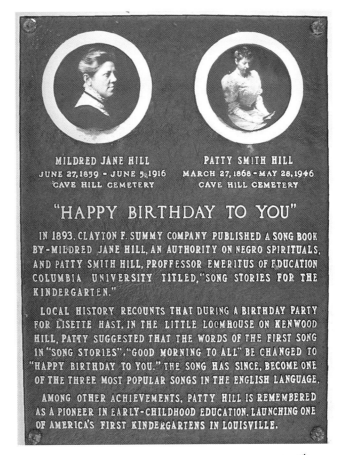

Photograph of the historic marker located in the "Happy Birthday" parking lot, under the 9th Street ramp to I-64, on Main Street, is courtesy of Rosemary McCandless.

Hill House

Possum Path was once the home to one of Louisville's most interesting historical sites which happened to be one of the oldest structures on Kenwood Hill, Hill House. Hill House was a log cabin built in 1893. It was located just south of the Little Loomhouse. The logs, at a glance, were very similar to life size "Lincoln Logs". They were notched on the ends and the notches fit snugly together. Chinking was placed between the logs to seal the gaps. The chimneys were made of stone. Hill House has been dubbed the Happy Birthday Cabin because it was once the summer home of Patty and Mildred Hill, two sisters who are credited with writing the song, *Happy Birthday.*

Mildred Hill was born in 1859. She began her career as a kindergarten teacher but later focused on her talent as a composer and concert pianist. Mildred was a musical scholar with a specialty in Negro spirituals. Patty Hill was born in 1868. She graduated from the Kindergarten Teachers in Training College in Louisville, Kentucky. Patty was considered a progressive kindergarten teacher for her time. She thought the classroom learning experience could be enhanced by keeping the atmosphere joyous. She believed in teaching by song. In 1893, Patty held a workshop at the Chicago World Fair. Her workshop drew participation from over 3,000 teachers. Patty's career eventually led her to Columbia University where she became the first woman to receive the Honorary Doctorate.

It was also in 1893 that the Hill sisters first published *Song Stories from the Kindergarten and Primary Schools.* The publication included a tune called *Good Morning to All* composed by Mildred, lyrics by Patty. *Good Morning to All* was developed as a song for teachers to sing to their class each morning to welcome students to the classroom. It did not take long for students to welcome their teachers to the classroom with the song, changing the words to, *Good Morning Dear Teacher.* The lyrics to this fun song went through yet another evolution during a birthday celebration for Lysette Hast, sister of Etta Hast, neighbor of Mildred and Patty, living at the Little Loomhouse. Lysette's birthday celebration was taking place at the Esta Cabin of the Little Loomhouse when Patty suggested the words to *Good Morning Dear Teacher* be changed to *Happy Birthday to You* and the rest is history.

Happy Birthday is noted by the Guinness Book of World Records as one of the most commonly sung songs in the English language. It is grouped with other popular songs, *Auld Lang Syne* and *For He's a Jolly Good Fellow.* Perhaps the most infamous performance of *Happy Birthday* was by Marilyn Monroe when she did a sultry rendition of the song to President John F. Kennedy at his Madison Square Gardens birthday celebration in May of 1962. It is also fun to note that *Happy Birthday* was sung by the crew of Apollo IX on March 8, 1969 and as a result is credited as being the first song sung in space.

During the 1960s, Hill House once again became a center of creativity when Lou Tate, then owner of the Little Loomhouse complex, partnered with Hal and Kitty Tenny, then owners of Hill House, to host the Midsummer Arts and Crafts Fair. The event included folk art weaving displays at the Little Loomhouse and paintings strung on clotheslines across the Tenny's patio. Musicians with acoustic guitars perched on the Tenny's roof, filling the air with song. A tradition was born. Soon, residents of the Hill and artisans from all around anticipated the bohemian get togethers.

Musicians, artists and patrons enjoy the Midsummer Arts and Crafts Fair at Hill House. Photographs are courtesy of Lee Ebner.

Photograph of Hill House is courtesy of the Tenny Family.

Over time, more and more development took place on Kenwood Hill. The removal of vegetation and altering of the land disrupted the natural water flow, setting erosion problems into motion. Several of the earlier structures on Kenwood Hill lost their foundations. Hill House was one of the victims. At one time, the cabin was stabilized only by its stone chimneys. Hal Tenny revisited his former home in the 1980s. He

commented about its dilapidated state, "We had no luck in persuading the developers to fix it, so, we had to move out". Eventually, the cabin was deemed a lost cause and torn down to make way for new construction. One lifelong resident of Kenwood Hill commented, "No one knew it was coming down, it was there one night when we went to bed, and then it just was not there any more."

Photograph of the interior of Hill House is courtesy of Nadine (Ryle) Oakley.

Devil's Backbone

At the top of Kenwood Hill lies a long exposed section of rock (as seen in the aerial photo). This rock is known as Devil's Backbone. It is believed that the Cherokee Indians camped on the land at the bottom of the hill. They were hunting buffalo which came to the numerous salt licks in southern Jefferson County. The top was a viewpoint to watch for the buffalo. The limestone outcropping of Devil's Backbone was used to dry their animal hides. Susan Harris tells of how one time when her older siblings went up on Devil's Backbone they met a man there who told them he was an Indian. He said that his ancestors had called it Sunshine Hill because of its exposed rocky top.

In 1864 the Phillips' Family sold what was then known as Cox's Knob, (Kenwood Hill), to Benoni Figg. Mr. Figg operated a lumber and charcoal business and a stone quarry on the hill. The quarry was Devil's Backbone. By 1893 Mr. Figg had sold off most of his land. With the purchase of Iroquois Park in 1888, the subsequent construction of the Grand Boulevard, (Southern Parkway), and the extension of the Fourth Street trolley line past Churchhill Downs, down Third Street, the area of Kenwood Hill began to be settled. At first many of the homes were summer cabins for people to escape the heat of the city. Gradually the area changed. In the 1930s, the Kenwood Park Residence Company began selling building sites.

Devil's Backbone photograph is used with permission of the University of Louisville Photographic Archives.

Early on the people, especially the children, of the area discovered Devil's Backbone. It was a wonderful place to explore. The view from the top was breathtaking. You could see the city to the north and miles stretched out around you on all sides. There were Indian arrowheads to be found. Fossils, remains of an ancient sea, were right at the surface of the rock. A series of trails developed over time. Although there were rumors of a long ago cave that had been perhaps blasted shut, no one ever found one. Some liked to tell the story that the hidden cave was haunted and you could hear the wind howling in it. If you got too close it might just suck you in. Many of the children living on the north slope of the hill would cut across the top to get to Auburndale Elementary School on the southern side. It was much closer than going around. It was also a favorite hangout for the teenagers. They would hike to the top and meet their friends.

1931 aerial view of Kenwood Hill, with north at the top of the photograph. Exposed rock is Devil's Backbone. Photograph is courtesy of Daryl Hamrick, James W. Sewall Co.

Mr. Lonnie Ray shared a personal remembrance of Devil's Backbone. In the 1930s, he was 15 years old. He and 10 or 12 of his friends at the Cabbage Patch Settlement had heard stories of the Devil's Backbone. One summer they decided to go check it out for themselves. They packed some food, a few tarpaulins for sleeping on and caught the trolley at Sixth and Magnolia. They got off on Kenwood Drive at the trolley's end and hiked up the hill. They spent the whole weekend there exploring. They saw foxes, raccoons, opossums, squirrels, and snakes. They had such a good time they returned to camp several other weekends that summer. They continued the tradition for several years until they reached an age when it no longer interested them. Mr. Ray still remembers the fun they had on those weekends.

The construction of homes on Kenwood Hill finally reached Devil's Backbone in the 1960s. Builders, Mr. William Eckles and his father, Mr. T.G. Eckles, set their sights on the top of the hill with the motto "Devil's Backbone or Bust". Eventually Devil's Backbone became covered with homes, and streets.

Today Devil's Backbone may be hidden from view, but the memory of what lies beneath those homes lives on. Many residents still recall hiking to the top, maybe taking a picnic lunch, and hunting for fossils and Indian arrowheads. The remains of the old stone quarry can still be seen with names and initials carved into the rocks. Reminders of a past that is still not forgotten.

Photographs of the old Kenwood Hill quarry, April 2006. Below is an Indian Arrowhead found by George Ray in the 1950s on Kenwood Hill. Top photograph is courtesy of Stefanie Buzan, left and lower photographs are courtesy of Rosemary McCandless.

The Street Car Line

"The End of the Line" is a common term for the last stop on a streetcar or trolley line. For the Fourth Street Car Line in Louisville's South End, the end of the line was known as the turn-around located at the corner of New Cut Road and Kenwood Drive.

Photograph of the Street Car Loop at Kenwood Drive and New Cut Road, current site of the Republic Bank, is used with the permission of the University of Louisville Photographic Archives. Iroquois Park is in the background, with Sunny Hill Pavilion visible in the distance. To the left, across Kenwood Drive is Senning's Park, now Colonial Gardens.

The initial end of the line was located at Churchill Downs, however, when Sam Stone Bush built his home on Kenwood Hill, he made arrangements through payment of subsidies to have the Fourth Street Car Line extend beyond Churchill Downs to Kenwood Drive and New Cut Road. The one fare route, using electric traction technology, became operational July 2, 1892. Additionally, Mr. Bush had the main roadways graded.

The Street Car made a stop along the route at a station located at Sixth Street and Woodlawn Avenue, courtesy of Mr. S. A. Lyon. In 1893, Mr. Lyon purchased a Pre-Civil War home along with 300 acres of land at Bellevue Avenue and Woodlawn Avenue. The Lyon family only lived in the house during the summer months, the remaining portion of the year they resided at the Seelbach Hotel. Mr. Lyon built the station to serve as a shelter for his two daughters to wait for the Street Car while residing at their country home.

Mr. George Pierson remembered that a Mr. Hennis ran Hennis Bus Service that picked up folks at the Kenwood Trolley Stop and would deliver them to their homes.

The electric traction streetcars were the first of their kind in the United States. Owned by Central Passenger Rail Road Company, the cars were "barned" at 1723 West Walnut.

3rd Street Trolley car with Kenwood Hill in the distance; photograph used with the permission of the University of Louisville Photographic Archives. The caption on the back of the photograph reads, "Running Northbound, six month old 1054 has stopped at Seneca Trail on Dec. 2, 1926. Even as late as 1926 it is evident that the area was sparsely populated, and yet a ten minute headway was provided."

The Kenwood Village Trolley Stop was located at the northwest corner of Esplanade Road and Third Street. This photograph shows a trolley headed south on Third Street, towards Kenwood Drive. It is used with the permission of the University of Louisville Photographic Archives.

Irma Atwell

Photograph of Irma Atwell and Robert Wadlow is courtesy of Irma Atwell.

When Irma Atwell initially arrived on Kenwood Hill, her husband, Woody, was not sure if she would last in the somewhat rural area due to the lack of modern conveniences. Irma has made her home on Kenwood Hill for the past 57 years.

Anyone who knows Irma will tell you that she is not shy. In 1937, Irma and her mother, Daisy Crosier were visiting a cousin, Unus Schueler in Alton, Illinois. Unus was taking Irma and Daisy on a site seeing expedition when she mentioned that they were coming up on the house of Robert Wadlow, the tallest man in the world- 8 foot, 11½ inches tall. Irma asked Unus to pull over when they arrived at his house. She got out of the car and knocked on Mr. Wadlow's door and asked him to come outside and pose for a picture with her. The above is the result.

CHAPTER 2

Historical Homes

**SS Bush House
The Kenwood
230 Kenwood Hill Road**

SS Bush (1864-1934) was the son of Sam Stone Bush, a notable Kentucky attorney and Cornelia Wheat-Bush, the first woman elected to public office in Kentucky. He was raised in Louisville and attended the Kentucky Military Institute. On October 21, 1886, SS Bush married Mary Allen. Together they reared four sons; Sam Stone Jr., George Allen, Monroe and Alexander.

It is interesting to note that George Allen and his wife Grace gave SS Bush his first grandchild, Carolyn. Carolyn Road was named in honor of Carolyn Bush.

During his lifetime, SS Bush prospered in many areas; real estate entrepreneur, owner and operator of railroad and power light properties in Georgia and Tennessee, financier of Louisville's first modern day office building, (the Starks Building), and publisher of The Southern Magazine are among some of his finest accomplishments. Today, the residents of the Iroquois Neighborhoods are still enjoying the fruits of Mr. Bush's labors and what was perhaps his greatest contribution to Louisville, the initial development of the South End.

Above, a young Sam Stone Bush. Left, SS and Mary Bush with their grandchildren, at their home on Kenwood Hill. Carolyn is seated on the far right. Photographs are courtesy of Paula Weglarz and the Berry Mansion.

In the 1880s, Bush became an associate of R.T. Coleman. By 1890, the two had launched the Coleman-Bush Investment Company with Bush serving as the Vice-President and Treasurer. The Coleman-Bush Company developed large tracts of land between Churchill Downs and Iroquois Park. This included Kenwood, Oakdale, Highland Park and Beechmont.

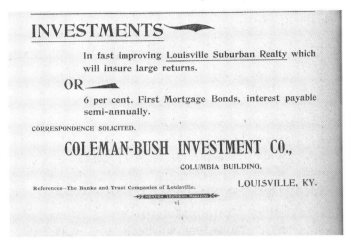

Advertisement for Coleman-Bush Investment Company is taken from The Southern Magazine 1894.

Mr. Bush retained a large parcel of land in the Kenwood Hill area for his personal use. The current Little Loomhouse site and surrounding acreage were included. Bush remodeled the Esta Cabin and built the Wisteria and Tophouse Cabins to form what is recognized today as the Little Loomhouse complex. In 1893, SS Bush hired the prominent architectural firm of Maury and Dodd to design his personal residence at the end of the private road, 230 Kenwood Hill Road. The entrance to the drive is flanked by two stone columns. In his youth, Alexander Bush fondly referred to the columns as eleven and twelve. When his parents asked him when he got in the previous night, his response was, "between eleven and twelve".

Sam Stone Bush Residence constructed 1893. Photograph is courtesy of Linda Masterson.

In an effort to add convenience and beauty to the area, SS Bush brought the Trolley out to New Cut and Kenwood Roads and lined the Grand Boulevard (Southern Parkway) and Third Street with Pin Oaks.

In addition to his own home, SS Bush also built notable homes for members of his family on Kenwood Hill; his mother's home, the Cornelia Bush House, and his sister's home, the Cornelia Gordon House.

The SS Bush House is a two story, shingle style, Dutch Colonial with a massive sandstone foundation. The stone was quarried on Kenwood Hill. The first floor of the house is one-and-one quarter inch cedar clap-board siding, the second floor is cedar shake shingle. During the 1980s, the National Register of Historic places gave the then owners permission to cover the entire house in vinyl siding in an effort to preserve it. The current owners removed the vinyl siding in 2006 to restore the home to its original state, once again revealing the Dutch Hex Sign on the front apex of the double gambrel.

The rear of the house contains a Flemish style library with hand-crafted windows which were made by inserting round pieces of glass into lead sheets. The glass is often referred to as wine bottle bottoms; however, Design Service of Louisville, KY, has identified them as roundels, an art glass that originated in Europe.

Library of SS Bush House, Christmas 2004. SS Bush purchased the fireplace mantel and the roundel windows while traveling in Europe. Photograph is courtesy of the Buzan Family.

Since 1938, the SS Bush House has shared the private road with three other houses. After SS Bush's death, the Burke family acquired the residence. They built three additional houses on the drive for their children. The cottage style houses are very similar in design. Due to the fact that each house on the private road belonged to someone in the Burke family, each house adopted the 230 address. The collection of Burkes in such a concentrated area led the neighborhood kids to refer to the area as "Burkeville". To this day, each house has retained the 230 address, which serves as a constant source of confusion for guests and delivery people.

Pillars referred to as Eleven and Twelve prior to construction of Burke houses. Photograph is courtesy of Sandy (Bush) Supinger.

Photograph of the private drive to the SS Bush house and the three houses that share the 230 Kenwood Hill Road address (Burkeville) is courtesy of Irma Atwell. Mrs. Atwell's home is in the top left hand corner, right behind the Bush House and carriage house.

The SS Bush House was placed on the National Register of Historic Places in 1979 by the Bouvette family. Today, the house is 113 years old and undergoing a much needed extensive renovation by the current owners, Tony and Stefanie Buzan. The Buzans hope to one day reconstruct the three story carriage house that once stood where the modern day garage stands today. If one looks carefully, they can see a portion of the original foundation of the old carriage house in the back yard.

Photograph of SS Bush's sons with their wives and children, on the side porch of the SS Bush House is courtesy of Sandy (Bush) Supinger.

**Cornelia Gordon House
308 Kenwood Hill Road**

Photograph courtesy of Stefanie Buzan December 2005.

The style of this National Register of Historic Places home is fairly eclectic, being a blend of Federal and Colonial styles. It is likely the home was originally built as a summer retreat. According to the 1879 Atlas of Jefferson and Oldham Counties, only two structures existed on Kenwood Hill at that time; the Esta Cabin of the Little Loomhouse, and 308 Kenwood Hill Road. At that time, both properties were owned by Charles Gheens.

The National Register of Historic Places nomination application describes the structure as being built in two sections. The front section circa 1875 was a one-story double pile frame structure with an open, central dog trot and hipped roof which set up on cedar posts. The dog trot provided ample ventilation.

In 1890, Charles Gheens sold the property to the Kenwood Park Residential Company. Sam Stone Bush was the secretary of the company. Mr. Bush personally purchased several parcels of land. The Little Loomhouse property and 308 Kenwood Hill Road were included in the purchase.

The second section of the house, the front porch, rear section and board-and-batten siding were added in 1894, when Mr. Bush called upon his friend, architect William James Dodd to redesign 308 Kenwood Hill Road as a residence for Mr. Bush's sister, Nellie and her husband Fulton Gordon and their daughter.

Nellie was an attractive young woman who caught the eye of Archibald Dixon Brown, son of then Governor, John Y. Brown. In late April of 1895, Fulton received word of a meeting between Nellie and Archie. Fulton acted on the information and found both Nellie and Archie in a rented room in a house on Madison Street. It is disputed that Archie fired the first shot; but nonetheless, Fulton shot and killed both Archie and Nellie. After a controversial trial and acquittal, Fulton disappeared. Their daughter was raised by her aunt and uncle, Mary and George Berry of Frankfort.

Photograph of Nellie Bush Gordon with her daughter, Cornelia Gordon Roberts, circa 1892, is courtesy of Paula Weglarz and the Berry Mansion.

The property at 308 Kenwood Hill Road passed to Sam Stone Bush's son, George and his wife Grace. George and Grace had two children, George Allen "Buz" and Carolyn. Carolyn was Sam Stone Bush's first grandchild and Carolyn Road was named in her honor. Buz recalled that his parents employed a live in maid named Claire Parker. Claire made $7 a week and was only off a half day on Thursday and a half day on Saturday. Buz has fond memories of going door to door singing Christmas Carols with his neighborhood friends, the Harris and the Fowlers.

Photograph of George, Grace, Anne and Monroe Bush on Kenwood Hill is courtesy of Sandy (Bush) Supinger.

The house remained in the Bush family until 1950 when it was purchased by Leuna and Dr. Pat Lyddan. The Lyddan's chronicled their personal history on the tiles around the fireplace. The tiles commemorate such things as the birth of their two children. After Mrs. Lyddan passed away, the home was purchased and used as rental property. Sadly, historic features were damaged through bad stewardship. The property once again serves as a private home since it was purchased by Robin Amsbary in 2004.

As with other older structures on the hill, this home has been damaged. Due to the shifting topography affiliated with the change of water drainage and weight affiliated with construction that occurred in the 1960's, foundation cracks and shifting are the results. The current owner is concentrating on structural stabilization, restoration of many of the exterior features and modernization of the infrastructure to preserve the home.

Cornelia Bush House
316 Kenwood Drive

High on Kenwood Hill, situated on four rolling acres, you will find the historic Cornelia Bush House. Cornelia Bush, daughter of Judge Zacharia Wheat, was born in Shelbyville, KY in 1834 and was often referred to as one of the most intelligent and spirited women in Kentucky. As the state librarian, Cornelia became the first woman to hold an elected office in the state of Kentucky.

In 1894, Cornelia's son, Sam Stone Bush, built her a home at 316 Kenwood Drive. The home was designed by prominent architect, WJ Dodd. Dodd drew much of his influence from his association with McKim, Mead and White during the 1893 Columbian Exposition in Chicago. This major national architectural firm, which promoted the Colonial Revival style, was commissioned to design the addition to The White House in Washington, D.C. A semi-circular porch was part of that design. It is likely that Dodd borrowed the porch design from McKim, Mead and White and incorporated it into the design of the Cornelia Bush House.

Cornelia Bush photograph is courtesy of Paula Weglarz and the Berry Mansion.

As a result of the striking resemblance between the Cornelia Bush House and Washington D.C.'s White House, the Cornelia Bush House has become known locally as the Other White House.

Cornelia Bush House shortly after construction, photograph courtesy of Sandy (Bush) Supinger.

The interior of the Cornelia Bush House features many of the original elements, preserving the sense of time and place from which it descends. Spanning above the front door, a fan shaped semi-elliptical window features thirteen circular prisms that are indicative of the thirteen original colonies.

Close up of sunburst window in entry hall of Cornelia Bush House, photograph is courtesy of Stefanie Buzan.

The house originally included seven fireplaces. Today, five fireplaces remain, one of which encases a recessed Madonna and Child, one of two pieces arriving in this country from Europe in the late 1800s. Three of the fireplaces are part of a triangular design sharing one chimney. The only other triangular design known to exist in the United States is in the Governor's Mansion in Virginia.

The Bosemer family was responsible for putting the house on the National Register of Historic Places. Linda Savage, former resident of the Iroquois Neighborhood recalled trick-or-treating at the Cornelia Bush House at the time it was owned by the Bosemer's. She recalled walking up the long, wide staircase that was on the front of the house. By the time the kids would get their candy and descend the stairs, the Bosemer's had positioned people under the stairs to jump out and scare the kids.

Photograph of Madonna and Child fireplace recessment is courtesy of Stefanie Buzan, 2005.

Ree Lomax, the current owner of the Cornelia Bush House has gone to great lengths to restore and maintain the historical integrity of this home. Although her work has uncovered many discoveries, she has yet to uncover the original use of a very well hidden trap door located in the floor of one of the bedrooms.

Alexander Bush House
303 Kenwood Hill Road

In 1927, the notable wedding of Miss Sally Lovell, daughter of Mr. and Mrs. C. Norman Lovell of 82 West Wyoming Avenue, Melrose and Mr. Alexander Bush, son of Mr. and Mrs. Sam Stone Bush of 230 Kenwood Hill Road, Louisville, Kentucky took place at the First Congregational Church of Melrose in Melrose, Massachusetts.

The bride wore a period gown in duchesse satin with a Queen Elizabeth collar, trimmed with net and pearls and a satin train, trimmed in pearls. The flowers in her bridal bouquet were of roses and lily of the valley. The maid of honor wore a gown of period taffeta in three shades of blue while two of the bridesmaids were dressed in green and two in a pea colored material. The bridesmaids carried bouquets of old fashioned flowers.

At the church, the candelabra were trimmed with smilax, and at each pew stood long candles along the path of the bridal party. The church was decorated with evergreen trees banked about the altar where more candelabra stood.

Photograph of Sally (Lovell) Bush on her wedding day is courtesy of Sandy (Bush) Supinger.

Meanwhile, on Kenwood Hill, in Louisville, Kentucky, construction plans were underway for the house the couple would call home. Within sight of the SS Bush residence, Alexander's aunt and uncle, George and Mary Berry (of the Juniper Hill/Berry Mansion in Frankfort) gave the new bride a house as a wedding gift to welcome her to the family. The house is located at the corner of Kenwood Hill and Bush Roads.

The Alexander Bush House is a two story, wood frame cottage. The lap board siding is of now extinct red poplar. The house features a stone sidewalk, chimney and entrance columns, all made from stone that was quarried on Kenwood Hill. The original blue prints for the house have been handed down from owner to owner and currently reside with the Rice family. The blueprints show the original structure prior to any remodeling.

Alexander Bush House 2005, photograph is courtesy of Lee Ebner.

APPRAISALS   RENTALS

Alexander Bush
REAL ESTATE
MARTIN BROWN BUILDING

OFFICE   RESIDENCE
JA. 3714   MA. 3902

Alexander Bush business card, courtesy of the Rice Family.

Alexander began working with Sam Stone Bush on a neighborhood development titled Kenwood Village. After his father's death, Alexander continued the development with the successful Alexander Bush Realty Company. The Alexander Bush House remained in the Bush family until Sally Bush's death in 1977.

The children of Alexander and Sally Bush are Lovell Bush and Sandy Supinger. Lovell is a 55 year veteran of Churchill Downs, having been through all positions including pari-mutuels. Sandy has been involved with medical facilities- her last one before retirement was 14 years of hospital management as Director of Patient Services.

Above photograph of Alexander Bush is courtesy of the Rice Family.

Left photograph of Sherman Crosier at Carolyn Drive is courtesy of Irma Atwell

KENWOOD VILLAGE

ALEXANDER BUSH

— IN CHARGE OF SALES —

Suite 306 Martin-Brown Building

AGREEMENT TO PURCHASE

ALEXANDER BUSH, *Agent*
Louisville, Ky.   Louisville, Ky._____192___

The undersigned hereby agrees to purchase the following property in Kenwood Village Subdivision,

Jefferson County, Kentucky, Lot No._____Block No._____and Lot No._____Block No._____

For the consideration of_____ $_____

The terms to be $_____down; $_____in_____months, $_____

in_____months and $_____in_____months, and the balance of

$_____, on or before ten (10) years from date, with interest at six per cent per annum,

payable quarterly, subject to all taxes after 192_____.

Deposit $_____   Deal to be closed_____192_____

Deed to be made to_____

_____

Remarks:_____

_____

Deed to be delivered upon the payment of 40% of the total purchase price.   This purchase is made with the understanding of and subject to the restrictions as per Deed Book 1230, Page 140, recorded in Jefferson County, Ky., Clerk's office, which will be part of the contract and deed for said property.

                                                              Purchaser

Accepted:
S. S. BUSH, *Owner*
By

_____
          Agent

*Left:
Photograph of
original
agreement to
purchase
property in
Kenwood
Village is
courtesy of the
Rice Family.*

*Below:
Photograph of
Lovell, George,
Alexander,
Monroe and
George (Buz)
Bush, is
courtesy of
Sandy (Bush)
Supinger.*

THE ENTRANCE TO KENWOOD VILLAGE

The Facts About
KENWOOD VILLAGE

The Beautiful New Subdivision of the Iroquois Park Section

 OTIS & BRUCE~INC.
INCORPORATED
312 South Fifth Street
City 2100

Front cover of a 1926 brochure for Kenwood Village is courtesy of Linda Masterson.

A View of Part of Kenwood Village

These Ten Points About KENWOOD VILLAGE **Will Surely Interest You**

What Is Back of Kenwood Village

1 Otis & Bruce, Inc. are turning their attention to the Iroquois Park district—a significant fact in view of their many successful, high-class subdivisions.

The Location

2 Kenwood Village is at the foot of beautiful Kenwood Hill, near Iroquois Park, facing Seneca Trail and the National Highway, a 60-foot boulevard.

3 It has a wonderful natural setting and to this will be added the skill and experience of master subdividers who will make it one of the finest home sections of Louisville.

Investment~ Profit~

4 No subdivision in Louisville has ever had greater possibilities for rapid increase in values. It is reasonably priced at the start, and the development work, which will begin at once, is so complete and in such skilled hands that its quick and growing appeal will be certain.

5 The terms, which are listed below, are undoubtedly the most remarkable for the purchaser in the history of Louisville's subdivision developments.

As a Place In Which to Live

6 Kenwood Village already has many beautiful homes, and the restrictions are in keeping with the value of the land. You will find, upon investigation, as beautiful home sites as are to be found any place in Louisville.

7 There is street car service running from the heart of the city directly through Kenwood Village.

8 The school facilities are excellent and within a few blocks of the Village.

9 The improvements listed below will start at once and are guaranteed in the sales contract and deed. These are the things that make the location of your home beautiful and comfortable:

 Paved streets
 Cement sidewalks
 City water
 Electricity
 Surface drainage sewer
 Street lighting standards
 Special planting of additional trees and shrubs

10 A maintenance fund is provided for fourteen years, for the proper upkeep of the gutters, surface sewerage, streets and parkways, the cutting of grass on vacant lots, and the care of trees, shrubs, and flowers.

UNPARALLELED TERMS

10% down---10% six months---10% twelve months

and no additional payments required on the principal for TEN YEARS!

How much do you suppose this beautiful property will increase in value by 1936—*ten years from now?*

OTIS & BRUCE~INC.

INCORPORATED

Center page of the 1926 brochure for Kenwood Village is courtesy of Linda Masterson.

Center page of the 1926 brochure for Kenwood Village is courtesy of Linda Masterson.

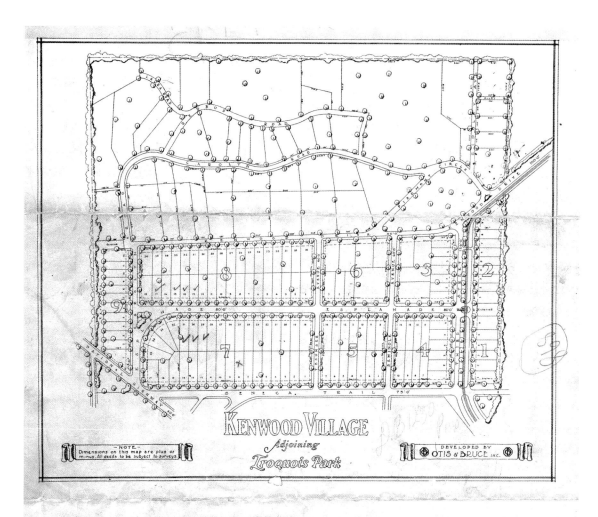

KENWOOD VILLAGE

Adjoining

Iroquois Park

—NOTE—
Dimensions on this map are plus or
minus. All deeds to be subject to surveys.

DEVELOPED BY
OTIS & BRUCE INC.

To Appreciate Kenwood Village You Must See It~

DIRECTIONS—Drive out Southern Parkway to Iroquois Park, turning left in the park. Take the first
Park Exit on the left, driving directly down KENWOOD BOULEVARD to the entrance.

By STREET CAR take the Park via 3rd car, and get off at KENWOOD VILLAGE.

OTIS & BRUCE·INC.
INCORPORATED
Developers and Agents
312 South Fifth Street

Back cover of the 1926 brochure for Kenwood Village is courtes of Linda Masterson.

Grahndale
5311 Lost Trail

The first home built on the west side of Kenwood Hill was built for the Grahn family and named Grahndale. The date of construction is unknown; however, Dora Jeane Hanley, a former owner of Grahndale, recalls while upgrading the electrical, she and her husband, James, discovered inspection papers tucked behind the original fuse box dated 1894. They decided to leave the paperwork intact.

Grahndale photograph is courtesy of William Hendricks.

Originally, the access to Grahndale was a road off of Kenwood Drive. It was the driveway to the property. The drive ran along the east side of Grahndale. When the land was subdivided, the lot was made smaller and the driveway was shortened and moved to the west side of the house. Today, the original driveway to Grahndale remains a closed off access alley that runs between the properties at 444 Kenwood Drive and 500 Kenwood Drive. Modern day access to Grahndale is via Lost Trail.

In 1930, the Hendricks family moved into Grahndale. They moved from New Jersey due to William Hendricks' job with Brown and Williamson. There were three Hendricks children, William Jr., James and Arthur. A fourth child, Grace, was born in the house in April 1935. Arthr Hendricks recalled, "Perhaps my favorite story of or move to Louisville happened the morning after we arrived from New Jersey. We arrived after dark. Early the next morning, Mrs. Harris came to our back door with hot oatmeal for the family. (They were the closest neighbor; I estimate now that their house and ours were about 100 yards apart across a gully between the houses). That began a friendship between the families that lasts to this day."

In 1954-1955, two of the Hendricks children, Arthur and Jim, began construction of the houses around Grahndale. They developed the road we know today as Lost Trail. At the time of development, the road was christened Hendricks Road; however, a resident that moved to the extension of the road objected to the name and was successful in a petitioning to have the name changed Lost Trail.

Dora Jeane Hanley recalled a story told to her by another previous owner of Grahndale: The lady of the house was home alone when suddenly a squirrel dropped down the chimney. Terrified and uncertain of what to do, she called the police who rushed over, entered the house and shot the squirrel with a .38.

Grahndale has been through a series of changes over the years to accommodate the needs of the owners of the time. When Grahndale was originally constructed, there was a bedroom on the first floor that included a sun porch. The Hendricks family removed the wall between the bedroom and the sun porch and added new windows and walls to create one large room that they used as a dining room. The carpentry work was completed by a neighbor on Fay. His name was Niles. Today, the current owners, the Cucullu family,use the same room as a master bedroom. Amidst the changes that have taken place in and around the house over the past 100 years, Grahndale has remained beautiful for all of the families that have called it home throughout the years.

The Hendricks Family, clockwise from left – James, Dad (William R.), Elizabeth, Arthur, Grace Hendricks Conlon, and mother (Grace), in the former Grahandale dining room, photograph is courtesy of Arthur Hendricks.

The Delph House
425 Kenwood Drive
Current site of DeSales Catholic High School

At the corner of Kenwood Drive and Laughlin Avenue, where DeSales High School now sits, was once the Delph family farm. The house was a two story frame topped by turrets and two brick chimneys. The yard was full of trees and surrounded by a wire fence with a wooden gate at the southwest corner. Although Mrs. Katie Figg Delph, her daughter Dicksie, and their home are no longer here, their memory lives on in the minds and hearts of some of the long time residents of the area. Dr. Irvin (Eddie) Bronner shared his memory of her yard full of many beautiful daffodils. He says she never minded you digging up some bulbs as long you filled the holes back in with dirt. Mrs. Mary Ellen Clements remembers the sheep that Mrs. Delph raised on her farm. Mr. Bill King remembers helping to shear those same sheep. He also states that the house with its turrets made many of the neighborhood children think that it might be haunted. Mr. George (Buz) Bush remembers that the ladies kept to themselves and you rarely saw them.

Photograph of the Delph House just before demolition with DeSales High School in the background is from the DeSales Freshman Yearbook, 1957.

In late 1940 Janice Johnson interviewed Mrs.Katie Delph as part of her English 101 class for Dr. Elva Lyon at the University of Louisville. Mrs. Delph was 80 years old at this time. She reminisced about her family and her husband, Richard W. Delph. Her husband's father was John Milbank Delph, the mayor of Louisville during the Civil War.

Photograph of Iroquois Park from Fay Avenue, circa the 1930s is courtesy of Mary Ellen (Rateau) Clements.

Mrs. Delph was the daughter of Benoni Figg. Mr. Figg owned 300 acres of land he had purchased from the Phillips family in 1864. This land was part of a land grant to Jenkin Phillips by the state of Virginia before Kentucky was a commonwealth. Mr. Figg's land included Cox's Knob, (now called Kenwood Hill), Kenwood Village and part of Burnt Knob, (now Iroquois Park).

According to Mrs. Delph, this land was virgin forest when her father purchased it with no roads or houses. Since there were so many trees, Benoni Figg built a sawmill near a creek on his property and sold the lumber to pay for the land, bragging that he got more for the timber than the land cost. Smaller timber was used for making charcoal. Lou Tate once recalled people talking about the eerie fires on the south side of the hill where the charcoal was made. Benoni Figg also built Strawberry Station on the Louisville and Nashville Railroad to ship his lumber to the city. The old Third Street road was built by him to make it easier to get to Beechmont. He used stone slabs he quarried from the area known as Devil's Backbone on Kenwood Hill. Kaufman's Department Store and the Broadway Baptist Church were also built of this stone. He built the Esta Cabin of the Little Loomhouse in 1870 as an office for his business. In 1876 he sold the cabin and several large tracts of land to Charles W. Gheens, the husband of his daughter, Mary Figg Gheens. They used the cabin as a summer house. Although they would later sell the cabin to Sam Stone Bush, much of the land would remain in the Gheens family for nearly a century.

Photograph of the remains of the old stone quarry on Kenwood Hill, March 2006, is courtesy of Rosemary McCandless.

With the Panic of 1893 Mr. Figg lost all his town property. All he had left was the 300 acres south of the city. He moved his family into a house on a hill adjacent to Kenwood. During this time Benoni Figg began selling off his 300 acres. Mr. Sam Stone Bush bought part of Kenwood Hill and Kenwood Village. A part of the land by Iroquois Park was sold to Mr. Oswald. Mrs. Delph and her husband bought several acres at $300.00 an acre to help her father. They built their house on this land. Mrs. Delph said "in those days this was the most Godforsaken country she had ever seen." There were no lights, gas or city water. The Bush family and a few others were the only ones living there.

Mrs. Delph was much younger than her husband and outlived him by a number of years. They only had one child, a daughter named Dicksie (after her father, Richard). Dicksie never married and was known in the neighborhood as quite a character. She was remembered to wear trousers and take care of the sheep, even doing the shearing. She was very protective of her sheep. It was recalled that one time when a sheep was missing, Dicksie showed up at a neighbor's party demanding to see the neighbor's dog, Skippy. She wanted to see if he had wool in his teeth. It was also remembered that Dicksie had poor eyesight. One time Mrs. Delph and Dicksie won a car. Dicksie would drive it with her mother telling her where to go.

In 1955 the archdiocese bought the land. The house was torn down and DeSales High School was built. Mrs. Delph would be surprised to see that Kenwood Hill is now part of the city that was once so far away.

Photograph of the Northeast view of the city from the top of Kenwood Hill, March 2006, is courtesy of Stefanie Buzan.

Orchard Hill
The Tafel House
The "Goat" House

The large, three story, brick house at 500 West Kenwood Drive has a very interesting history. The property was originally part of the large tract of land owned by Benoni Figg. In June of 1908, Ann Juriah Figg, the widow of Benoni Figg, sold the land to the Columbia Trust Company. The land apparently sat vacant for the next 12 years. On November 13, 1920, Joseph and Helen Ivins bought the real estate from Columbia Trust Company. They built the beautiful brick home that still stands today. The home was completed in 1921 and Mr. and Mrs. Ivins lived there until 1925.

500 West Kenwood Drive 2005, photograph courtesy of Lee Ebner.

On February 25, 1925, Mr. and Mrs. Ivins sold the property to Mr. and Mrs. Paul C. Tafel (Mary). Mr. Tafel owned Tafel Electric Company. The Tafel family lived in the city on Boulevard Napoleon and decided they wanted to live in "the country". The property sits on a small hill at the base of Kenwood Hill. This small hill is Orchard Hill. The family always referred to the house as the "Orchard Hill House." At the time that they moved in they had three children; Paul, Mary Elizabeth (Betsy), and Patricia. Three more children were born to the family while they lived at the house; Mary Doherty, William (Bill), and John (Jack). Around 1930 Mrs. Tafel's father, Dr. William Doherty, came to live with the family. A downstairs bedroom was added on the back of the house for him.

Orchard Hill was a wonderful place to live. The family had two ponies, Gaity Boy and Captain, for the children to ride. On the west side of the house was a hedge. Through the opening in this hedge was a path lined with roses. At the end of this path was a large circular pool. On hot summer days the children and their friends would play in the pool. On the other side of the pool was a large, white pergola with wisteria growing on it. Mrs. Susan Harris Wilburn, who grew up in the area, still remembers how beautiful this garden was.

Dr. Doherty with his grandchildren, Paul, Mary Elizabeth, Patricia, Mary Doherty, Bill and John (Jack) in the living room at 500 West Kenwood Drive. Photograph is courtesy of Bill Tafel Sr.

Tafel children with family ponies and in the garden pool, photographs courtesy of Bill Tafel Sr.

Since this house was built long before air conditioning, a sleeping porch was built off the second floor. Mr. Bill Tafel remembers having sleeping cots on the porch and the family sleeping out there. Senning's Park Zoo was right up the street. Sometimes you could hear the lion roar at night. Mrs. Wilburn also recalls how every now and then one of the animals from the zoo would get loose. It was pretty exciting.

Mr. Bill Tafel also recalls one spring when he was seven years old, he wanted a bicycle. He decided to raise chickens to pay for it. He said that he raised a couple hundred chickens in the carriage house on the property. He had to feed water, and clean up after them. His Grandfather Doherty helped him keep track of his expenses. He then made a deal with Mr. Snider of Iroquois Gardens Club to buy the chickens. After selling the chickens he had enough money for the bike and some left over to put in the bank. He decided to make more money by using the bike for a paper route. He had the bike only a short time when he flipped the bike over on the rocky road by the Bush's house, (Kenwood Hill Road), wrecking it beyond repair. He still has the scar from the accident. The next year when he suggested he might like to try raising some hogs to make money, his mother said, "no way". He remembers his sister Betsy raised some homing pigeons.

Tafel Electric Company was a distributor for Westinghouse. Periodically the executives from Westinghouse would come to town and Mr. and Mrs. Tafel would entertain them at Orchard Hill. Mr. Bill Tafel remembers that they usually wanted to go to Churchhill Downs. On Derby, a group of executives from Pittsburgh, PA, would take a Pullman Railroad Car and arrive Derby morning. Some of the family would meet the train and bring them out to Orchard Hill. Everyone would be dressed up, sipping mint juleps and enjoying a brunch. Mr. Tafel says it was quite an affair. They would then take them to the Derby and afterwards take them to the station at 10th Street and Broadway to return to Pittsburgh.

In the summer of 1942 the Tafel family moved from Orchard Hill. The next person to live in the house was Mr. James J. Dunn. He lived there until 1951 or 1952. A couple of those years he rented the carriage house apartment to Mr. Clinton B. Harr.

In the early 1950s the house was purchased by Mrs. Ethelyn Duckwall Steinaker McCree. Mrs. McCree raised several goats during her time there. The goats were very special to her. When she made out her will in 1960 she provided for her one remaining goat,

Sugah. After her death the property was put in a trust with Citizens Fidelity Bank. Sugah had quarters there on the property and those quarters were to be maintained for the goat until her natural death. The property was to be rented in order to provide income so that Sugah could have adequate care. A caretaker was also to be provided for Sugah. The estate could not be sold until the death of the goat. To this day there is a mound in the yard where the goats are buried.

The goat shed at 500 West Kenwood Drive was destroyed by fire during the 1970s. Photograph is courtesy of Gloria (Brockman) Montgomery.

Mr. Tom Atwell, who grew up on Kenwood Hill, remembers the goats at the house at 500 West Kenwood Drive. When he was a boy there were two or three large goats (full sized - not dwarf goats), that were kept in the field behind the carriage house of the property. Miss Booker who lived there took care of the goats. He remembers that the older lady (Mrs. McCree) of the house had no children and treated the goats as if they were her children. One of the other neighbors, Mrs. Gloria Brockman Montgomery, recalled hearing the ladies singing the goats to sleep in the evenings.

There was a large apple tree in the goats' pasture area. Mr. Tom Atwell recalls one time he and some friends decided to get some apples from that tree. They no sooner got to the tree when one of the big goats took offense at their trespassing in his pasture and started charging at the boys. The boys took off for the fence as fast as they could. They were so scared that they climbed quickly through the fence, ripping their clothes and getting numerous cuts and scratches. Once they reached safety on the other side of the fence, they turned and only then noticed that the goat was on a large chain and could not have gotten them. The boys had to laugh at themselves. The goat had earned his apples that day.

In October of 1967 Dr. and Mrs. Edward J. Brockman (Marguerite) bought the property from the estate of Ethelyn Duckwall Steinaker McCree. The pasture land was used for the children's pony and horses. The house was remodeled as four apartments.

In the summer of 2005 the land was divided. Mr. Charles Hayes bought the section of the property with the house. He is currently restoring the house to a single family home.

Photograph of the Carriage House at 500 West Kenwood Drive 2005, is courtesy of Lee Ebner.

The Harris House
Formerly located at 206 Kenwood Hill Road

During the time that Kenwood Hill was predominately farmland and wilderness, A. B. and Susan W. Harris and their five children, Harriet, Mary Walton, Bright, Tyree and Susan lived in a wooden home set amongst the trees. One side of the home was adorned with large, French windows. Susan Harris Wilburn fondly recounted some of her favorite childhood memories of the home.

Photograph of the Harris House is courtesy of Susan (Harris) Wilburn.

"Several people in the neighborhood had gardens which had to be ploughed each spring. Ours was a big garden with an asparagus bed which ran the length of the garden."

"Andy lived on Strawberry Lane. He had two mules, a plow, a harrow and a disk-everything needed to prepare the ground for planting. The day Andy came to plough was an exciting day. I guess it was the disk we got to ride on. What fun! Also, sometimes an arrowhead would be brought from its hiding place to the top of the ground."

"The hard work Andy did was remarkable! He was hunchbacked with one leg much shorter than the other. When he stood, it was on one leg with the other resting on the longer leg's calf. He had one of the most beautiful and kind faces I've ever seen- dark brown eyes which expressed all kindness and gentleness. Andy took good care of his tools and equipment and beautiful care of his mules. They were as gentle as he."

The old Harris house sat vacant for a number of years and fell victim to disrepair. It was eventually demolished. Today, the Burke family lives at 206 Kenwood Hill Road. On the land where the Harris house once stood, the Burkes have built a home of their own in the beautiful park like setting.

The Harris children enjoy growing up on Kenwood Hill. Photograph is courtesy of Susan (Harris) Wilburn.

A Letter from David C. Fowler to Susan Harris Wilburn

Dear Susan,

Thanks very much for your letter and the invitation to send some remembrances from our childhood in the vicinity of Kenwood Hill. Like you, I have recollections of an enjoyable life in those days but I don't have an actual record to pass on to you. I might suggest that there is an account of the discovery of the French burial stone published in one of the Louisville Male High School magazines (the Spectator). I took some liberties in writing that but it was based on a real discovery by my brother Bill and one of his neighborhood friends. The school ought to have a complete file of that magazine.

You might also recall the famous barn in the woods at the foot of Kenwood Hill, which we thought was haunted. One night we formed a task force of Fowlers, Bushes and I think also some Harrises to sneak up there one evening and see what we could find. In the dark, we approached the barn and were paralyzed to see a light shining from the inside and this was followed by ominous sounding noises within. We all ran to our homes and hid from whatever person or thing we feared might come and get us. Only later did we learn that the threatening goblin was none other than the benign Mrs. Bush- least likely to have been suspected.

Kenwood Hill was itself a place for much exploration, not the least being, "the Devil's Backbone" and a huge tree near the back-side on the way down toward Auburndale (our school). There were a few homes on the slopes occupied by people with little tolerance for invaders intruding on their privacy. We had to beware of their dogs and my brother Bill was seriously bitten by one of those. But the Hill was a place much loved by us all as a place for exploration.

Susan, I'll bet you could come up with some exploration of your own, after all, you and your family lived on a forested slope not far from the Hendricks. I hope you will be able to tell some good stories from those days. Thanks for keeping those memories alive. Meanwhile I will sign the form sent to me in case you want to offer my bits and pieces above to the Preservation group. Sorry I don't have any pictures. All the best to you and your family. It's been too long since we have seen you all.

Love from all of us out here,

David C. Fowler

Hickory Grove
5400 Hickory Hill Road

Prominently situated at 5400 Hickory Hill Road stands a large, two story, pre Civil War home. Its construction is of logs. The design suggests that three separate cabins were merged to create the structure that is known today as Hickory Grove.

The exterior logs are covered by board, batten and weatherboard. The interior log walls are either exposed log or covered with plaster. The previous large dog trots have been transformed to serve as an entry hall and a dining room. The house boasts five fireplaces, three of which are constructed of hand cut stones.

The cellar features a large concrete vault. The original intent of the vault remains a mystery. There is speculation that it was perhaps used during prohibition. The current owners, Herb and Linda Phillips, have converted the vault into an impressive wine cellar.

Hickory Grove fall of 2005, photograph courtesy of Stefanie Buzan.

Hickory Grove boasts two great pieces of Kentucky History. In January 2006, the Grove was gifted with "fancy work" from the estate of Maria Vogt. The collection of vintage linens is one of the finest in town. Maria was originally from Germany but was a long time resident of the South End.

In the main hallway of Hickory Grove, the Phillips house a second piece of Kentucky History, a spinning wheel that once belonged to the family of Elias Newton Hutchenson of Butler County, KY. In the late 1800s, Elias married and had four children (two boys and two girls).

One day, Elias' wife was brushing their daughter's hair by the fire. Her long skirt caught on fire. She panicked and ran for help across the field to the next farm where her mother-in-law and father-in-law lived. She never made it as she died en-route.

Elias re-married to Emily Susan Hutchenson. She was fifteen when they married. Elias was thirty-seven. Elias' father made his new daughter-in-law the spinning wheel that the Phillips have today. Elias' two daughters from his first marriage lived with Elias and Emily; however, the two boys were sent to live with other relatives. It is believed that the boys were sent away as they were close in age to Emily. In fact, one of the boys was the same age as Emily (15).

Elias and Emily went on to have seven children of their own. The boys from Elias' first marriage never came back to live with the family. They remained with relatives and visited their sisters and step-brothers and step-sisters often.

One of Elias and Emily's daughters, Ruth, lives in Louisville. She still remembers helping her mother with the "cotton cards" (two paddles with short bristles used to clean the wool). Even though the sheep were washed before they were sheared, some leaves and dirt remained in the wool. Ruth also remembers the "bats" (collections of individual wool strands). Ruth would hold the "bats" for her mother until her small arms ached. Her mother would allow Ruth to rest her arms periodically before the spinning continued. The wool was used for socks, gloves, sweaters, and hats for the family.

Hickory Grove evolved when CP Raquet was awarded a 15,000 acre land grant in 1785. The three original log cabins are believed to have been constructed in the 1820s, during the time that Raquet owned the land.

In 1831, John H. Fenley purchased 800 acres from Raquet's heirs. By 1841, Fenley acquired additional surrounding property, giving him a total of 1,100 acres. Upon John Fenley's death, the property was passed on to his son, Isaac. By 1858, the property had taken on the identity of Hickory Grove. The road we know today as Park Boundary Road, located at the southern most corner of Iroquois Park and New Cut Road, once served as a private lane to Hickory Grove.

Photograph of the side view of Hickory Grove, January 1956, is courtesy of Dave and Mary Winges.

Annie Fenley inherited the house and the 54 acres surrounding it upon Isaac's death. Annie sold the private lane, and another 6.5 acres of land to the Board of Park Commissioners for absorption into Iroquois Park. This is the section of the park known as Fenley Woods.

In 1903, Annie Fenley moved to California. At that time, Hickory Grove and its land passed from the Fenley Family for the first time in 72 years. The acreage was sold off and developed into the neighborhood it is today.

Lustron Homes

The Iroquois Neighborhood is fortunate to have two of the rare and unusual Lustron Homes. One is located at 121 Cambridge Drive and the other at 7238 Southside Drive.

The Lustron Home came about as a result of a housing shortage facing the United States as the soldiers were returning home from World War II. Carl Strandlund was the Vice President of Vitrolite Corporation which manufactured porcelain, enamel, steel panels. The panels were customarily utilized for gas stations, however, Strandlund recognized the opportunity to give the panels a new life- prefabricated housing. Hence, the Lustron Corporation was born.

Housed in an old aircraft plant in Columbus, Ohio from 1948 – 1950, the Lustron Corporation built 2,498 homes over a two year period at a cost of $6,000-$10,000 to the consumer. It took 400 factory hours to complete an unassembled Lustron. Upon factory completion, 3,000 pieces were loaded onto a specially designed Fruehauf truck (big and yellow) and delivered to the permanent location. Upon arrival, it typically took an additional 300 on site hours to assemble a Lustron.

Lustron Home loaded onto the truck for delivery.
Photograph used is courtesy of Bill Kubota at KDN Films.

Each Lustron Home had a steel frame and porcelain coated panels on both the interior and exterior. The steel walls enabled the homeowner to hang pictures and such to the walls with magnets. The initial Lustron floor plan was a 1000 square foot design with two bedrooms. The exterior color provided choices for the home owner, pink, tan, yellow, aqua blue, green or gray and the interior beige or gray. More than not, the Lustron homes that are standing today still bear the original roofs and siding along with built in wall cabinetry.

Today, Lustron homes are an endangered species. Hundreds of them have fallen victim to demolition. As a result, steps are being taken to develop programs to preserve these wonderful and unique homes.

Top: Lustron home located on Cambridge Drive.
Bottom: Lustron home located on Southside Drive.
Photographs are courtesy of Stefanie Buzan.

William James Dodd

The Kenwood Hill area of the Iroquois Neighborhood is home to four properties that are on the National Register of Historic Places; the S.S. Bush House, the Cornelia Bush House, the Cornelia Gordon House and The Little Loomhouse. Three of the four properties were given historic status in part due to the architect who designed them, William James Dodd.

William James Dodd was born in Chicago, Illinois in 1862. He graduated from the Art Institute of Chicago. While in Chicago, Dodd enjoyed apprenticeships with some of Chicago's most influential firms, working on projects such as the Manhattan Building and the town of Pullman, Illinois. In 1884, at the age of 22, Dodd moved to Louisville, Kentucky.

Dodd began his first partnership in Louisville with O. C. Wehle. It was simply called O. C. Wehle and W. J. Dodd. The firm was in business from 1887-1889. After the partnership with Wehle dissolved, Dodd entered into a partnership with Mason Maury, hence, Maury and Dodd. It was during this partnership that Dodd began designing personal residences on Kenwood Hill. It was uncommon for Dodd to build in what was at the time the rural South End area, however, Sam Stone Bush was a personal friend. As a result, Dodd was delighted. He designed Mr. Bush's personal residence at 230 Kenwood Hill Road, Mr. Bush's mother's residence (Cornelia Bush House) at 316 Kenwood Drive and the redesign of an old cabin for Mr. Bush's sister (Cornelia Gordon House) at 308 Kenwood Hill Road.

Over the course of his career, Dodd went on to design some of Louisville's most famous and influential commercial buildings, places of worship and residences, some of which are the Seelbach Hotel, the Filson Club, the Presbyterian Theater and Office Building (known today as Jefferson Community College Downtown Campus), Fourth Avenue Methodist Episcopal Church, First Christian Church, St. Paul Episcopal Church and the Louisville Country Club.

While on a European tour, Dodd contracted a fatal illness and passed away unexpectedly. He was sixty-eight. He left behind his wife, Lone Estes Dodd but no children. If you would like to learn more about W. J. Dodd, visit Christopher White's website at: **http://home.earthlink.net/~hdrctw34/index.html**

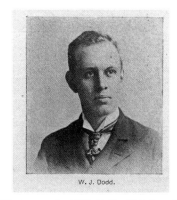

KENNETH McDONALD AND
W. J. DODD, ARCHITECTS
600 EQUITABLE BUILDING
LOUISVILLE, KENTUCKY

Photograph of W. J. Dodd taken from   *W. J. Dodd business card is courtesy of Humana Inc.*
The Southern Magazine, 1894.

Kenwood Hill Athletic Club
Contributed by Bill Hendricks

The Kenwood Hill Athletic Club was formed in the late 1930 s by the young men (actually still boys) of the neighborhood. Football and baseball were the featured sports and the athletic fields were in a large open area immediately across the Hendricks private road from the Tafel garage. This long gone athletic field has been replaced by the large Bedford stone house at 444 West Kenwood Drive.

The baseball field featured a large tree not too far behind second base and an infield that more resembled a newly-plowed field than a baseball diamond. The outfield duties were precarious since the area was also used to pasture cows.

The football field had a dry-ditch running through it with numerous crawdad mounds that made end-runs precarious at times. The star of the football team was Crutcher Allen. He was ably assisted by:

Bu Bush	Bright Harris	Bill Hendricks
Paul Tafel	Tyree Harris	Jim Hendricks
"Pluto" Rateau	Bill Fowler	David Fowler

Other neighborhood pickups filled the ranks on occasion, and Mary Walton Harris chipped in when the situation became desperate. Susan Harris was the official water-girl.

The football team engaged the Beechmont Athletic Club, the Inverness gang and other local teams. The win-loss record is lost in obscurity which is a blessing.

The baseball team was more successful, but the last season ended abruptly when the baseball was lost in Mr. Harris garden.

Photograph of Susan (Harris) Wilburn and Arthur Hendricks on Kenwood Hill is courtesy of Susan Wilburn.

CHAPTER 3

Iroquois Park

OUTLOOK POINT, IRIQUOIS PARK, LOUISVILLE, KY.

COURFIELD & SHOOK
47435

Iroquois Park

In 1890, in the aftermath of a tornado torn Louisville, an organization of civic minded business men calling themselves the Salmagundi (a spicy dish of conversation) lobbied throughout Louisville to gain support for their vision of preserving the beauty of the River Valley through a network of parks.

The concept was met with a great deal of enthusiasm from the community. A system consisting of three parks was decided upon. The land necessary for what is known today as Shawnee and Cherokee Parks came together rather quickly. In 1889, Mayor Jacobs bought a 300 acre parcel of land known as Burnt Knob and sold it to the city as a park. It was named Jacobs Park in his honor. Mayor Jacobs circumvented the civic initiative, hence the park's nickname, "Jacob's Folly". In retrospect, Mayor Jacob was successful at securing a portion of the future location of the 739 acre Iroquois Park as part of what would become the Olmsted Park Network.

In 1891, the Salmagundi were successful in engaging Fredrick Law Olmsted, Father of American Landscape Architecture, to solidify their vision. At the time, Olmsted was sixty-nine and working and living at the Biltmore Estate in Ashville, North Carolina. It is interesting to note this was the same year Olmsted was involved in the Columbian Exposition in Chicago that resulted in his work on Chicago's Lakefront.

Vintage photograph of Iroquois Park is courtesy of the Olmsted Conservancy.

Olmsted thought that all development design should connect people simultaneously to the land and each other. True to his teaching, Olmsted developed the infrastructure of each park highlighting their natural assets, because he realized, like the boulevards that would connect them, they would grow and change over the years. Creating access to the parks through narrow roads that curve naturally with the land, Olmsted made nature accessible without altering it. Iroquois Park consists of rustic, wooded terrain that allows the park goer to escape their urban confines. The road that connects Iroquois Park to the city was 150 feet wide and known as The Grand Boulevard. The Boulevard was originally made from packed dirt and had to be watered regularly to keep the dust down. With a bridle path on one side and a bike path on the opposite, the Grand Boulevard would grow into what we know today as the majestic Southern Parkway.

Left: Postcard depicting the early, unpaved, Grand Boulevard (Southern Parkway). Below: Vintage picture of the Iroquois Park South Overlook. Both are courtesy of the Olmsted Conservancy.

Iroquois Park has changed significantly from the days when folks came out to picnic and frolic and commune with nature. Some of the mainstay activities are still available, such as golf, tennis and basketball. Some modern day activities have been added to the park such as the extensive Frisbee golf course.

The riding stables are no longer a part of Iroquois Park; however, the Louisville Metro Police Mounted Patrol board their horses in the former park stables.

From April 2nd through October 28th, the road to the top of Iroquois Park is open on Wednesday, Saturday and Sunday, from 8:00 a.m. to 8:00 p.m. thus limiting access to the top of the park to pedestrian traffic during the closed time. The park has adopted a policy to allow trees and plant life to grow naturally which has resulted in overgrowth at the lookouts. The view from the northern lookout where patrons once parked to enjoy the view of the city from one of Louisville's highest elevations is now obstructed by vegetation. The Parks Department is making a conscious effort to protect the ecology of the Park. Eventually, the large trees will stabilize the hillside, enabling grooming of the underbrush, thus allowing the park goer to enjoy the view.

Photograph of Police Officers in Iroquois Park, May 2006, is courtesy of Stefanie Buzan

A view from the Iroquois Park Northern Overlook in 2005, photograph is courtesy of Stefanie Buzan.

The amphitheater is a huge draw during the summer months however; gone are the days of dressing in your finest clothes to see up and coming stars. Today's patrons enjoy the plays in much more casual attire.

Physical Characteristics of Iroquois Park
Contributed by Alan Nations

Iroquois Park is made up of about 676 acres of mostly forested land. Beneath these woodlands lies a foundation made up of primarily New Albany shale of Devonian Age. The soil is highly erodible. A mantel of loess, a windblown glacial deposit, covers the

knobs and slopes of the forest. Much of the uneven-aged intact second growth forest can be considered "old growth". Very large trees, along with numerous dead snags and fallen logs scattered throughout the park, are abundant evidence of natural tree gap regeneration that has continued over a very long period of time. Iroquois Park is a unique geological and ecological landscape.

Photograph is courtesy of the Olmsted Conservancy.

Vintage postcard is courtesy of the Olmsted Conservancy.

In 1897 a general plan for the park was drawn up by the landscape architect firm of Fredrick Law Olmsted. Mr. Olmsted's plan was to design a scenic reservation, to be conserved and made accessible and enjoyable, rather than dramatically changed. Mr. Olmsted's plan also sought to provide the visitor a sense of separation from the urban surroundings. This was accomplished by maintaining mixed woody borders and increasing the density of the park's woodland edges. Today the park retains all of its original features.

A Road in Iroquois Park, Louisville, Ky.—35

Vintage postcard is courtesy of the Olmsted Conservancy.

A walk on one of the many trails will take you through old growth woodlands with towering American beech, red oak, white oak, yellow poplar, shag bark hickory and sugar maple trees. The under story is made up of dogwood, spice bush, green briar and pawpaw. On the rich organic woodland floor in the lower areas, spring wild flowers form huge colonies and provide visitors a real show during April and May. On the slopes, serviceberry, redbud and dogwood trees bloom in otherwise dormant woods, signaling that spring has arrived.

There is an abundance of wildlife along the trails, including whitetail deer, gray fox, raccoon, opossum and box turtle. Owls can be heard hooting in the distance, and a variety of songbirds make their home in these woods.

Photograph of owl, April 2006, is courtesy of Rosemary McCandless.

Vintage postcard is courtesy of the Olmsted Conservancy.

The park's highest point, Burnt Knob, has four vistas that provide panoramic views of the surrounding area, including the city of Louisville. A savannah of native Kentucky warm season grasses and wildflowers covers a portion of the knob's south side. The savannah is beautiful in any season. A loop trail circles through it, giving the visitor an opportunity to step back in time and experience a landscape that once covered much of Kentucky. Several benches near small ponds are great places to sit quietly, listen to the chorus of frogs and truly commune with nature.

The natural areas of Iroquois Park are diverse ecological systems unique to this urban area and preserved in time. A natural jewel! This is the best kept secret in Jefferson County.

Alan Nations
Naturalist
Olmsted Conservancy

Photograph of a family of three red tailed hawks, July 2006, is courtesy of Garry McCandless.

Iroquois Wildlife

The Iroquois Neighborhoods are old and established; coupled with Iroquois Park; it is not uncommon to see a large variety of wildlife. From the furry to the feathered, see if you can spot the inhabitants listed on our check list. We even left a few blank spots for the over achiever.

◊ Squirrel
◊ Opossum
◊ Rabbit
◊ Chipmunk
◊ Raccoon
◊ Mole
◊ Deer
◊ Fox
◊ Snake
◊ Lizard
◊ Salamander
◊ Barred Owl
◊ Screech Owl
◊ Blue Jay
◊ Northern Cardinal
◊ American Robin
◊ Indigo Bunting
◊ Eastern Bluebird
◊ American Gold Finch
◊ Purple Finch
◊ Red-Tailed Hawk
◊ Red-Bellied Woodpecker
◊ Hairy Woodpecker
◊ Nuthatch
◊ Tufted Titmouse
◊ Variety of Warbler
◊ Mockingbird
◊ Mourning Dove
◊ Rock Dove
◊ Pigeon

◊ Mallard
◊ Baltimore Oriole
◊ House Finch
◊ Whip-Poor-Will
◊ Red-Winged Blackbird
◊ Snow Bunting
◊ Song Sparrow
◊ House Sparrow
◊ White-Throated Sparrow
◊ Yellow-Bellied Sapsucker
◊ Downy Woodpecker
◊ Red Headed Woodpecker
◊ Pileated Woodpecker
◊ Common Grackle
◊ European Starling
◊ Brown-Headed Cowbird
◊ Carolina Chickadee
◊ Chimney Swift
◊ House Wren
◊ Carolina Wren
◊ Rufus Sided Towhee
◊ American Crow
◊ Pine Siskins
◊ Common Flicker
◊ Ruby Throated Hummingbird
◊
◊

The Bridle Path

Southern Parkway had watering troughs and drinking fountains so both horses and pedestrians could cool themselves along the park like paths. Thelma Carter recalled a time in the 1940's when the riding stables were located on Southern Parkway where the Resurrection Episcopal Church is today, at 4100 Southern Parkway. "You could rent a horse by the hour. You would leave the riding stable, travel down Southern Parkway on the bridle path, turn around at Iroquois Parkway and go back to the stable. I was not a very good rider, so I always got a slow horse that usually ended up grazing a lot along the way".

As early as the 1920s, problems began to surface regarding the dangers of the horses sharing the bridle path with children on their way to school. A special meeting along with a tour of Southern Parkway was called to discuss the fact that two horses galloped through a group of school children and the horses' hooves left the turf a mess of water and mud. Such stirrings eventually lead to the demise of the bridle path. Southern Parkway maintained an active watering trough for horses at the corner of Marret Place and New Cut Road until the 1950s.

Photograph of Susan (Harris) Wilburn and Mary Doherty Tafel Barnum on the bridle path, circa the 1930s, is courtesy of Susan (Harris) Wilburn.

Jacob's Lodge

In 1929, the public got its first glimpse of architect Clifford P. Reichert's drawing for the rustic Jacob's Lodge located at the top of Iroquois Park. The original design included a spacious lounge with an open log fireplace and hewn brown rafters across the ceiling. The lodge was originally meant to serve as shelter for park goers in the event of bad weather. The cost of the structure in 1929 was $15,000.

By 1932, Jacob's Lodge had become a hot spot for church groups, family reunions, bridge clubs and schools. According to the Park Board in City Hall, the lodge was booked every night in November and December, through December 18th.

In a 1932 interview, E. W. Sutherland, pastor of Clifton Unitarian Church, gave us a glimpse into the activities going on at Jacob's Lodge, "Yes, indeed, we have come up here before and we always know we shall have a delightful time. We can hike over the hills or around the hill and then come back here for genial warmth and a bite to eat. We bring a lunch, but we supplement it with a little hot food cooked over the camp furnaces outside. It isn't necessary to tell you how much children and grown-ups too, enjoy roasting marshmallows and weenies over the hot coals. And they can also toast bread."

"And, it's a real pleasure to come because everything about this place is so spotlessly clean and every possible courtesy is extended to both the children and the grown people. The policy of the Park Board in regard to letting parties have the place exclusively within certain specified hours allows people to have the lodge for their own use. The place has become most popular. We know it as we have to make reservations very far in advance." Pastor Sutherland followed up with a summation of what his group would be doing at the lodge for the day, "At noon a party will be on hand. It gives way at 2 o'clock to a second party and a third one will be ready at 6 o'clock. Often three and four groups use the lodge and open air cooking ovens. Oh, and hiking parties sometimes take a moonlight walk and reach the lodge in time to cook supper and leave at 11:30 when the lodge closes."

In 2006, Jacob's Lodge is one of five indoor lodges in the Louisville Metro Parks system. It is available by reservation only at a public rate of $100 and a non profit rate of $70. The lodge is used for family picnics, employee appreciation days, weddings and field trips.

Photograph of Simms Family Reunion at Jacob's Lodge is courtesy of Margie (Simms) Gibson

Iroquois Amphitheater

In March 1938, the Board of Parks Commission approved the creation of a 3,500 seat; open air theater in Iroquois Park. Construction of the Iroquois Amphitheater began in April of 1938 and was complete in just 75 days. July 4, 1938, the Iroquois Amphitheater opened to a sold out crowd with a production of *Naughty Marietta.* Louisville's *Starlit Stage* was born. In 1938, Paul Beisman, Manager of the St. Louis Opera said, "Without a doubt, Louisville has the most beautiful outdoor stage in the world."

The stage came alive with operettas and Broadway musicals. Sets were designed by Rollo Wayne and the first permanent producing director was Frederick DeCordova of Johnny Carson's Tonight Show fame. The Amphitheater was the birthplace of the Louisville Chorus and over the next 60 years, the stage was graced by stars such as Audrey Meadows, Gene Berry, Don Ameche, Jeanette McDonald, Nelson Eddy, Carol Channing and Liberace. Vickie Doherty Martin, a longtime resident of the Iroquois Neighborhood remembers attending the Liberace concert, "Liberace invited everyone down to see all his diamonds, because he said we were paying for them".

Vintage postcard depicting the original Iroquois Amphitheater is courtesy of Rosemary McCandless.

Sixty years later, patrons of the Amphitheater fondly reminisce about the glorious place that has provided entertainment to one generation after the next. An evening at the Amphitheater meant fathers and their sons put on their coats and ties, mothers and their daughters put on their best dresses and white gloves. Young couples fell in love, married and returned to the Amphitheater with their children.

All three photographs showing the construction of the Iroquois Amphitheater by the WPA (Work Projects Administration), in 1938 are courtesy of the Iroquois Amphitheater Association.

Center photograph shows the lights for the water curtain.

During World War II, local merchants got together to support the war effort by purchasing Monday night tickets for the troops, for shows at the Amphitheater. There was instant chemistry between the chorus girls and the soldiers. For a period of time in 1941 and 1942, Amphitheater volunteers began arranging "chaperoned" dates between the chorus girls and the soldiers. It did not take long for Monday nights to become known as Victory Nights.

One of the main attractions at the Amphitheater was the dazzling, colorfully lit water curtain. The water curtain was originally designed to distract the audience from scene changes during a performance. The water curtain's popularity was only rivaled by its ability to attract mosquitoes. As a result, the water curtain was eventually scrapped.

A treat during intermission was a bottled orange soda, known as the Big Orange Drink, bottled by Bireley Bottling Company of Atlanta, Georgia. The drink's popularity was legendary. The Big Orange Drink almost seemed to have a cult following, which resulted in long lines during intermission. A trip to the Amphitheater was just not complete without the traditional Big Orange Drink.

Vintage ad for Bireley's Orange Drink.

In the fall of 2000, the original Amphitheater saw its final curtain call and the old structure was replaced by the new Amphitheater. The new Amphitheater is partially protected from the outdoor elements and boasts air conditioning, dressing rooms, offices and meeting rooms. The spirit of the *Starlit Stage* lives on and interest in the Amphitheater is renewed for generations to come.

Original program from the first show at the Iroquois Amphitheater.

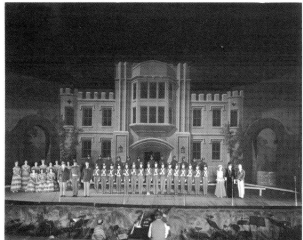

All four photographs are courtesy of the Iroquois Amphitheater Association. The first two on the left are of a dress rehearsal for Desert Song. The above photograph is of chorus girls getting ready backstage. The bottom photograph is of a performance of Vagabond King with a set designed by Rollo Wayne.

The Zachary Taylor Tree
The Daniel Boone Tree

In a June 29, 1912 newspaper article two historic trees in Iroquois Park are mentioned, the Zachary Taylor tree and the newly discovered Daniel Boone tree. The trees were both in the Fenley Woods section of the park, less than one-half mile apart. The Zachary Taylor tree was reported to be preserved from vandalism by a close woven wire fence. It was described as having a malignant fire scar at its base, overgrown by ivy and its top torn by storm. It was feared that the tree would not last much longer. The inscription read, **"Z. Taylor", "1835", "deer hunt".** The initial "Z" looked like the figure "3" which was characteristic of Zachary Taylor's signature. In contrast to the condition of the Zachary Taylor tree, at this time the Daniel Boone tree was described as in glorious condition.

The inscription on this tree was **"D. Boone. 1803. Kill a bar".** The Daniel Boone tree was believed to be authentic at the time of this article since it was ascertained that Daniel Boone visited Kentucky around 1803. He arrived by boat on the Ohio River and traveled the old Saltlick trail from Portland to Green River where he furnished evidence in a land suit.

Photograph of Zachary Taylor Tree used with permission of the University of Louisville Photographic Archives.

In the late 1920s the fate of both trees comes into question. The Zachary Taylor tree suffered from heart rot, a fungus that attacks and destroys the tree's heart wood. For six weeks four experts worked to save the tree. All the decayed wood was chiseled out. The remaining wood was then disinfected with dichloride of mercury and alcohol to kill any remaining fungus. Eighty feet of one inch steel rod was used in bracing the cavity which was then painted with waterproof paint. Approximately 12 tons of concrete was used in filling in the six inch sections, with each section separated by tar paper. The outside was painted with a wash to close the pores in the concrete and keep out dampness. It was believed that in time the bark would cover the filling, leaving the tree stronger and healthier than before.

In the early 1930s, after the Daniel Boone tree was struck by a lightning bolt, many wanted the Boone tree saved as the Zachary Taylor tree had been. When a tree surgeon was called in he found the tree to be 99% dead. The decision was made to take the tree down. In April of 1932 the sawyers first cut it off six feet above the ground, let the snag down gently and then butted off a four foot section with the inscription, leaving a two foot stump. The Filson Club promised to preserve the carving as long as possible. They still have it today.

Several years after the Filson Club took possession of the trunk, the authenticity of the carving came into question. Based on the tree rings and the fact that in the approximately 130 years from the time of the carving until it was cut down the bark would have had time to cover over the carving, it was decided that it was more than likely not authentic. Authentic or not, it is still a wonderful piece of history and part of the folklore of Iroquois Park.

Photograph of Daniel Boone tree is used with permission of the Filson Historical Society.

While the Daniel Boone tree was documented, the Zachary Taylor tree did not receive as much publicity. It was still in Iroquois Park when the Daniel Boone tree came down. At one time installing rustic seats and making the spot an historic shrine was discussed. An article on January 20, 1935 in the Courier-Journal tells that the tree had to be taken down. The foresters of the park board had decided that it was in grave danger of falling and was beyond saving. That same article says that the J.B. Speed Museum had recently acquired the part of the trunk with the carving. They were planning to treat the wood for preservation before it would go on display. Today the J.B. Speed Art Museum has no record of the tree and does not know what became of it. Its fate remains a mystery. Both trees are now part of the legends of the Iroquois Park area.

Photograph of the preserved Daniel Boone Tree at the Filson Club, July 2006, is courtesy of Rosemary McCandless.

For those curious about where the two trees stood, the June 9, 1929 Courier-Journal's "WHAS Trailfinder Girl" column gave the following log and directions.

The Trail Finder Girl appears over WHAS at 5:30 each Thursday afternoon:

THE TRAIL
The Courier-Journal and The Louisville Times Building 0.0
South on Third St. and Southern Parkway; turn left off Southern Parkway to Taylor Boulevard 6.1
Taylor Boulevard and Kenwood Ave. Turn into Park 6.7
Park Stables. Turn left 6.8
Stop for Zachary Taylor tree ... 7.7
Pass road at left; straight ahead 8.0
Dogwood Road and sentry house; straight ahead 9.1
Dead thorn tree; stop for Daniel Boone tree 10.5
Turn left 13.4
Southern Parkway and Taylor Boulevard 13.6
The Courier-Journal and The Louisville Times Building 19.7

Follow the log. When you stop .9 miles from the entrance you can see the Taylor tree from the road. It is about 150 yards from the park highway and you will recognize it by the large amount of concrete work that has been done on its trunk. The tree bears the inscription: "Z. Taylor, 1835, deer hunt".

One and three tenths miles beyond the Taylor tree is the location of the Daniel Boone tree. A dead thorn tree on the left edge of the road marks the exact spot for you to park your car. Walk directly off the road about 20 yards, past the thorn tree, until you come to a curve in the bridle path. The Boone tree is just off the curve in this path. You will recognize it because it is a topped beech. It bears this inscription: "D. Boone, 1803, Kill a bar".

Park Police / Golf Course

When Iroquois Park was created it was quite a distance from the city. There was a need for a police force to protect the parks and their visitors. In September of 1895 a city ordinance was passed authorizing a special police force for the parks. The uniform of the Park Guard was to be different from the city police. It was made of cadet gray cloth, with black welt on the coat and pants, and had park buttons. The badge was silver in the shape of an acorn with the words "Park Guard".

Mr. Bud Farmer, who grew up in the area during the Depression, remembers the Park Guard. His family lived on the old Marret farm, the current site of the Iroquois Golf Course. The Marret family cemetery is still there, between holes 1 and 10. If you're a good golfer you've probably never seen it. Two of the houses on Marret Place at the Southern

Parkway entrance to the park belonged to the Marret sisters. Eventually the Marret Estate was bought from their heirs by the city in the 1940s for the golf course. Bud Farmer remembers hunting in the area as a boy. He had to be very careful not to hunt in the park, but sometimes whatever he and his dog were chasing would decide to cross the road and enter the park. How frustrating to see your dinner escaping! Since the Park Guard strictly enforced no hunting in the park he then would have to make the decision of whether or not to follow it and take a chance on getting caught.

Photographs of the Marret Cemetery (in the Golf Course), and Marret Houses located on Marret Place, April 2006, are courtesy of Rosemary McCandless.

Another problem the Park Guard had to deal with was romantic parking in the park. Early on the Board of Park Commissioners drafted a rule prohibiting the parking of vehicles with "the curtains drawn". It's not known if this was written to apply to curtained carriages or early automobiles. In the late 1930s the Board asked that dome lights be lit when parking. Lookout Point in Iroquois Park with its view of the city in lights was a very popular spot. At midnight a patrolman would take out his flashlight and politely tell the occupants of each car that it was time to get going.

In 1941 the Park Guard was disbanded. Its officers were appointed to the Louisville Police Department. The parks are now patrolled by the Louisville Metro Officers in the area.

Left: Photograph of Woody Atwell, Park Police Officer, is courtesy of Irma Atwell.

Below: Aerial Photograph of the construction of the Iroquois Park Golf Course in 1946 is courtesy of Daryl Hamrick, James W. Sewall Co.

The Water Source at Iroquois Park

Many residents in the area did not get city water until the 1950s or 1960s. Most relied on cisterns to collect rain water or wells. In times of drought many found a need for water. The city provided water at Iroquois Park through a large faucet. Several residents of the South End and Fairdale remember coming here to fill large containers with water. Water trucks would also come here and fill their large tanks with water to deliver to people.

Photograph of water trucks at Iroquois Park. Used with permission of the University of Louisville Photographic Archives.

Bicycles

Iroquois Park and Southern Parkway have always been a favorite place to ride bicycles. No matter what the season you'll see people riding bikes. This tradition of riding bikes here goes back to the start of Iroquois Park and the "Grand Boulevard", (Southern Parkway), in the 1890s.

The Bicycle Parade

On October 8, 1897, Louisville hosted one of the largest bicycle parades in the South. It was in honor of the Board of Park Commissioners who had authorized the construction of a cinder bike path along Southern Parkway.

The parade route started at Broadway and followed Third Street to the Iroquois Cycle Club headquarters. The Club was located near where the Watterson Expressway currently crosses Southern Parkway. Approximately 10,000 cyclists took part in the parade with an estimated crowd of 25,000 to 50,000 spectators watching the event.

The cyclists were organized into 17 divisions, each one headed by 17 buglers on bikes and 7 mounted policemen. In order to coordinate the divisions the buglers of each division sounded a call as they went. Buglers stationed at the cross streets would return the calls. The bugle calls were also answered by a cannon being fired at the review stand located south of the Confederate Monument. According to a Louisville Times article the bugling and cannon fire could be heard for miles.

Many cyclists rode in costumes. Since the parade was at night many of the bikes were decorated with lights. One pair of tandems was decorated as a sailing ship with a 900 candlepower searchlight. Some of the women cyclists wore bloomers which were considered revolutionary at the time. The parade concluded at the clubhouse with a speech by W.T. Rolph urging the construction of more parkways.

Photograph of the Historical marker at Third Street and Southern Parkway, July 2006, is courtesy of Rosemary McCandless.

The Wheelmen's Bench

The Wheelmen's Bench is a limestone seat in Wayside Park, at the intersection of Southern Parkway and Third Street. There is an inscription that reads "Erected with the Approval of the Board of Park Commissioners by the Kentucky Division of the League of American Wheelmen in Memory of A.D. Ruff", followed by the year 1897 in Roman numerals. The story of how Southern Parkway came to have this bench is an interesting one. In June of 1897 the Wheelmen State Conference, (bicycles riders), received a $1,000.00 bequest from A.D. Ruff, $200.00 for a tombstone and in division money, and $800.00 for a memorial fountain. Wayside Park was actually the second choice for the fountain, but when the first site declined, it was chosen.

A.D. "Pap" Ruff had been one of the oldest and most enthusiastic cyclists of Kentucky. He was 69 years old at the time of his death and the oldest member of the League of American Wheelmen. A few years prior to his death he had made a journey awheel to Yellowstone National Park. An amazing feat for any man, let alone one of his age.

Enid Yandell designed the memorial. Groundbreaking took place on September 25, 1897. By January 17, 1898 the bench had been completed and the Courier-Journal reported that it was in use and would get lights and water when the season opened.

Photograph of the Historical marker at Third Street and Southern Parkway,
April 2006, is courtesy of Rosemary McCandless.

In the late 1970s and early 1980s, stones started to disappear, which opened the bench to weather. In 1982 the Metropolitan Park and Recreation Board ordered the bench torn down and rebuilt. Park Employees replaced some stones, but left the battered inscription as it was.

In 1984 the Louisville Bicycle Club took up the cause of the bench restoration with the idea of adding Wallace "Sprad" Spradling, a beloved former club president, to the memorial. Brummett Monument in New Albany volunteered to store the seat slabs and inscription stone at their facility. This temporary storage would last three years. Finding the correct replacement limestone proved to be difficult. Finally, Charlie Donohoe, of Charlies Wrecking, identified that the building he was demolishing (the Green Mouse Café at Third and Winkler), had the correct stone. Before it could be used, the city had to approve it, so Mr. Donohoe took it to his farm in Indiana for storage.

On October 30, 1998, Alloyce Black, the Louisville Bicycle Club President, presided over the dedication of the memorial. Mr. Brummett, Mr. Donohoe, Alloyce Black and other Wheelmen Members were not paid for their work. The presence of this monument is their gift to the city. It is a worthy memorial to two wheelmen.

Photograph of the Wheelmen's Bench located at Third Street and Southern Parkway, July 2006, is courtesy Rosemary McCandless.

Run For the Hills

Running has become a popular sport and pastime. Iroquois Park with its unique array of hills and flats has become a challenging, self-fulfilling running and walking course for many residents. The Kentucky Derby Week's Mini-Marathon starts at the park and includes much of the lower road in its course. The Midnight Chase was a popular race run at night in the park and on Southern Parkway for many years.

Photograph of The Kentucky Derby Mini- Marathon Starting Line, from the front of the crowd of runners, and the back of the crowd of runners, is courtesy of Stefanie Buzan.

Iroquois Hill Runners was started in 1978. The club hosts and promotes races. They offer some training sessions and informal group runs. Their Thanksgiving Day Race has run every Thanksgiving for the last 27 years. This 5 mile course runs to the top of the park and the runners pass four Olmsted designed park views.

Iroquois Hill Runners Logo

The current president of the club is Swag Hartel, a former British world class runner and a sub four-minute miler. He came to the United States in 1970 to attend, and graduate from, Western Kentucky University. In 1977 Swag came to Louisville to be a professional runner. He started selling shoes part-time in 1978 and two years later started his own store in the Auburndale Shopping Center. He now serves thousands of customers who have come for good shoes, good prices, and as Swag promises, the best service in town.

Swag Hartel initiated a new race in 2004, The Southern Parkway Mile. It consists of a series of one mile races down Southern Parkway from the park to Woodlawn Avenue. The race includes a neighborhood festival. It is currently being jointly sponsored by Swag Shoes, St. Mary and Elizabeth Hospital, and Furniture Liquidators.

Like Swag's running shoes, the Iroquois Hill Runners, and Swag himself, are a perfect fit for the park and the neighborhoods around it. They continue to support and contribute to the area.

Photograph of Mini-Marathon runners headed west, towards the park, on Kenwood Drive is courtesy of Stefanie Buzan.

CHAPTER 4

The Gardens of Iroquois

❖ *Senning's Park* ❖ *Colonial Gardens* ❖ *Iroquois Gardens Club*

Senning's Park

Carl Fredrick Senning found his way to Louisville from Kesse, Germany in 1868. On March 8, 1877, Carl Fredrick Senning and Minnie Goeper were married in the home of her uncle, Charles Goeper. This union of life endured 62 years, producing a lucrative business and six children.

Fred and Minnie purchased their first restaurant at 407 West Market Street. The venture lasted five years. Next the Sennings opened a restaurant and hotel on East 8th Street. It was at this location that the Sennings began introducing new experiences to their customers. They introduced Louisville to finger bowls in the dining room and the first bowling alley.

The Sennings continued to take advantage of new opportunities. As the streetcar reached out to South Louisville and the Grand Boulevard stretched to Iroquois Park, the Sennings too found themselves heading south, finally settling at Kenwood Drive and New Cut Road. Here they built Senning's Park and the Senning family continued to introduce Louisville to new attractions for the next four decades.

Photograph of Senning's Park is courtesy of William Senning Jr.

In 1920, William Senning took over operation of the park from his parents when they left for an extended visit with relatives in Germany. William carried on the family tradition of originality in Louisville when he opened the first zoo.

William Senning built one of the finest private collections of animals in the country. It included lions, tigers, bears, monkeys and a variety of exotic birds, just to name a few. William Senning acquired his animals through years of correspondence with other zoos and collectors. In a letter from the general manager of the Cincinnati Zoological Park Association, dated February 20, 1924, per Mr. Senning's inquiry, he was offered the following:

I have some black Fallow Deer, two year old, that I could price you at $120.00 per pair. Also one male Water Buffalo, a year old, very fine specimen, at $165.00. This is a very fine animal and would be quite an attraction in some show. Have one Lioness that I could price you at $450.00- seven years old, and very fine specimen. These are all the animals that I could spare just at the present time.

Photograph of William Senning Jr. is courtesy of William Senning Jr.

The following text from a circa 1927 news article announced the arrival of the ostriches at Senning's Park:

When manager Will Senning of Senning's Park Zoo purchased two young ostriches from the Florida Ostrich Farm, at South Jacksonville, Florida, he little reckoned that his young hopeful, William A. Jr., and probably thousands of other children in and around the city, would soon be in a fair way of becoming proficient in the art of ostrich driving. This form of sport has long been a favorite with the folks of Australia, the native habitat of these birds.

William August Senning Jr. was born in Louisville, Kentucky on June 7, 1925 to William August Senning Sr. and Ethel Gray Senning. In 2006, Bill Senning Jr. lent insight to the fact that the top floor of the main building was living quarters in which the Senning family lived. William Senning Jr., recalled it would get cold during the winter and the family would have to store the alligators in the basement of the main building to keep them warm.

Over the years, quite a collection of stories detailing animal antics at Senning's Park became legendary. One such story was recounted by William Senning Sr. regarding a time that Jimmy the Bear was fed so many ice-cream cones that he fell and could not get up. The Senning's Park staff had to throw a bucket of water on poor Jimmy in order to bring him back around. Mr. Senning also shared details of a strange animal that park officials were never able to identify. The animal was purchased from the stockyards for $150 and was described by Mr. Senning as beastly, big as a bull with a hump like a camel and feet like a deer. The animal managed to escape his cage and took off down New Cut Road. It was later found on the bank of Floyds Fork. Even though Mr. Senning offered a $50 reward to anyone who could identify the animal, he got no takers.

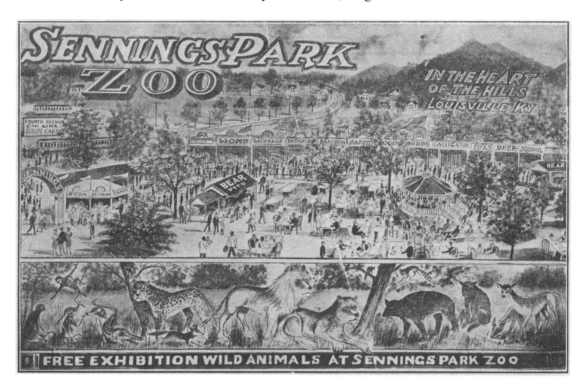

Photograph of a sketch of Senning's Park Zoo, later used as a postcard,
is courtesy of William Senning Jr.

In its heyday, the popularity of Senning's Park prompted the Louisville Street Railway Company to add cars to their service to Third Street and New Cut Road. For the observance of Decoration Day alone, the park reportedly prepared for a crowd of between eight to ten thousand people.

WILLIAM A. SENNING

IN THE HEART OF THE HILLS

A fragrant, beautiful eating-place. Cozily warm all winter under the palms. A well-cooked chicken, frog leg, baked duck or porterhouse steak dinner prepared by expert chefs and daintily served. A refined atmosphere that will greatly help you enjoy your meal. In the city, yet out of the noise of it. Such is the pleasure which awaits the diner at

 # SENNING'S PARK

1926 ad for Senning's Park

Throughout the years, Senning's Park attracted crowds seeking everything from five cent beer to dancing to highfalutin picnicking. In the February 1, 1940 edition of the Courier-Journal, the description of the average picnicker at Senning's Park was described as follows:

Picnic crowds at the park thirty or more years ago were out, supposedly, to enjoy a days car ride and frolic. They were dressed in the most voluminous and cumbersome finery. The men wore high, stiff collars and shirts with long sleeves and stiff cuffs. Their ladies wore yards and yards of white dress goods and broad hats balanced on top of the most elaborate coiffures. Probably their feet were in high buttoned shoes many sizes too small. Poor people! How could they enjoy a picnic rigged out like that?

Senning's Park was host to a number of political meetings. It has been said that four Kentucky Governors were nominated during political gatherings at Senning's Park. Esther Lillian Preston Perkins, former Iroquois resident and former Auburndale school teacher reflected on trips to Senning's Park with her family as a child. She looked forward to getting a bag of popcorn and looking at the animals in the zoo.

Photograph of a meeting (possibly political) inside Senning's Park is courtesy of William Senning Jr. Note the absence of women in the picture.

Photograph of Benefit Dance ticket is courtesy of William Senning Jr.

During the Depression Senning's Park fell on hard times. The animals were expensive to care for and feed. Bill Senning could no longer afford to maintain the operation. Fred and Minnie resumed operation of the Park. Fred and Minnie worked Senning's Park until after midnight, seven days a week. Minnie supervised the cooking while Fred bossed the bar. This continued until Fred Senning's death on December 6, 1939.

Senning's Park was sold, lock, stock and barrel to B. A. Watson for fifteen thousand dollars. B. A. Watson remodeled the property and named it The Colonial Bar and Grill.

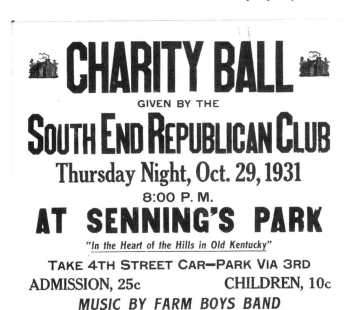

Louisville was fortunate that William Senning Sr. kept good notes on all of his animals, such as how to care for them, what to feed them, cost and source of purchase and various mistakes and successes he had with the animals. Around 1970 the James Graham Brown Foundation consulted with Mr. Senning as they prepared to start the current Louisville Zoo.

Photograph of Senning's Park Reproduction Souvenir poster is courtesy of Beverley Wheatley.

Colonial Gardens/Teen Bar

In 1940 BA Watson purchased Senning's Park for fifteen thousand dollars. He closed the zoo, remodeled the structure and renamed it Colonial Gardens Restaurant and Grill.

During the 1940s, Colonial Gardens hosted big band entertainment and dancing. It took on the persona of an evening club that included a full service restaurant. Over the course of BA Watson's ownership of the property, a couple of events took place at the club that kept local headlines interesting.

Aerial photograph of Colonial Gardens is used with the permission of the University of Louisville Photographic Archives.

In 1944, Colonial Gardens temporarily lost the right to sell rationed foods during a time of war due to application falsification. On January 13, 1948, police raided Colonial Gardens and seized an illegal Beat-the-Dealer gambling device. There were no arrests made. On August 16, 1950, some time after the last customer of the evening had gone, BA Watson noticed smoke coming from the eaves of Colonial Gardens. The building was on fire. Firemen were able to extinguish the flames. The fire damaged two dining rooms and there was smoke damage to Watson's apartment on the second floor. Although the damages were estimated at ten thousand dollars, Watson vowed that the fire would not disrupt business. The cause of the fire was unknown.

During the early 1950s, Colonial Gardens was purchased by Herm Schmid. Eventually it became known as Teen Bar. During this time, the club was strictly non-alcoholic. It was the favorite outing for many teens, especially those living in the South End.

The teens that patronized Teen Bar were thrilled to have such a wonderful hang-out. They developed a newsletter simply titled "*Teen Bar News*", in an effort to keep all of the "members" abreast of social highlights and events. The Teen Bar News staff consisted of the following:

EDITOR Dottie Carmen
SPORTS EDITOR Jim Fisher
TYPIST Lucy Rice
REPORTERS Caroline Drexler, Rita Wagner, Bobby Barlow, Al Curelle and Johnny Noon

In the editorial section of the newsletter, the paper staff expressed their appreciation to the management team of Teen Bar:

I think Al and Helen have done a wonderful job by starting the Teen Bar. They have gotten us a nice, decent, respectable, place where we can meet new friends and dance until our heart desires. We also want to show our appreciation to Herm. Herm, Al and Helen have really been working hard to get us everything we need and like. They want to satisfy all the teenagers. I know there isn't a finer Teen Age Club as "TEEN BAR". Believe me, they haven't stopped yet. Teen Bar in the future will be bigger and better. Any suggestions will be welcome. Our managers are three wonderful people. Let's do our best to show our wholehearted appreciation.

Teen Bar became widely known as the place to watch or participate in all of the popular dances such as the Jitterbug, Rat Race, Sailor Hop, Elephant Walk, Camel Walk, Bunny Hop, Dirty Boogie, Slow Dance and Hokey Pokey. Wednesday night was the ever popular Jitterbug contest, hosted by Ed Kalley.

Jitterbug Queen Caroline Drexler shows off her moves. Photograph courtesy of Caroline Drexler.

Some time around 1956, Carl Coons took over the Colonial Gardens property. He changed the name to Carl's Bar and operated it for about three years. It is a well known fact that Elvis Presley's grandparents lived at 4008 Beaver Street, just a few blocks North of Colonial Gardens. Although it is not a confirmed fact, local oral history dictates that in 1956, while in town for a performance at The Armory, Elvis spent the evening on Beaver Street with his grandparents. Some time that night, he made his way to Colonial Gardens and took the stage for an impromptu performance.

Photograph of the former home of Elvis Presley's grandparents, July 2006, is courtesy of Rosemary McCandless.

In 1959, Wilburn "Curly" Bryant began leasing the property and changed the name back to the original, Colonial Gardens. Curly operated Colonial Gardens until his death in 1983. At that time, his son, John Bryant, took over the operation.

Photograph of Colonial Gardens is courtesy of the Beechmont Branch of the Louisville Public Library.

In a 2005 interview, John Bryant reminisced about the way the building looked when his father acquired it. When you walked in the front door there was a beautiful, spiral staircase and banister leading to the second floor. Just past the staircase, you walked into a small piano bar and after the piano bar was the main bar. The bar is the original bar; the original dance floor was in the center. The staircase was removed along with the walls of the small piano bar in order to open up the floor plan. Eventually, John put in a new staircase to obtain better access to the second floor.

Throughout the years, Colonial Gardens underwent physical changes as well as changes to the genre it catered to. During the Bryant years, Colonial Gardens became known for its live entertainment. During the 1950s and 1960s, they hosted high school type bands such as the Sultans and the Monarchs. Things moved to a rock and roll theme in the 1970s and by 1978, a country/Urban Cowboy theme was heavily influencing the club. Over the years, some of the famous visitors to the Colonial Gardens stage included Billy "Crash" Craddock of "Rub It In" notoriety- who fell off of the stage during his performance and Angie Humphrey of local weather fame. John Bryant recalled hearing a story about Jerry Lee Lewis performing on the premises. In the story, Jerry Lee played a hot pink, baby grand piano. John never could confirm the details of the story. Years later, when the new staircase was installed to the second floor, a hot pink, baby grand turned up on its side was discovered in a closet on the second floor- a mystery as to how and when it was put there.

Colonial Gardens offered a little bit of entertainment for everyone. Activities upstairs in the loft included pool, darts, karaoke as well as a small bar; downstairs housed the dance floor, bands and main bar. A variety of dance lessons were offered. They tended to change from year to year as fads changed. Some of the most popular were the two step, waltz, line dancing and swing. It is interesting to note that the routine bar patrons were not the people who took the dance lessons.

Colonial Gardens memorabilia is courtesy of Garry McCandless.
Photograph, May 2006, is courtesy of Rosemary McCandless.

John Bryant pointed out the Colonial Gardens that his family operated was more of a night club/social gathering vs. a bar. John and some of his long term staff, Donna Eades, Jan and Julie always looked forward to the biggest night of every year- New Year's Eve. John recalled, "It was a whole new beginning, you would celebrate the same way, a new start. We had people who came there for generations to celebrate. They were not the normal bar crowd, they were people you would see once a year, get caught up on everyone and then not see them again until the next year. We always went all out. It was a special night".

As times changed, emphasis placed on driving under the influence of alcohol started to take a toll on all of the bars in the South End. Colonial Gardens went from being open seven days a week to four days a week. Eventually, there was insufficient business to keep it open. Colonial Gardens closed its doors to the night club business in June of 2003. A capacity plus crowd of over 600 people packed in to say good-bye.

The legacy of both Senning's Park and Colonial Gardens is an abandoned building at the corner of Kenwood Drive and New Cut Road; vacant and unused with a very uncertain future. Perhaps it may once again become a much needed social gathering place, an asset to the community or maybe it will be another landmark, pushed aside to make room for a new pharmacy or gas station. Only time will tell.

Photograph of Colonial Gardens, May 2006, is courtesy of Stefanie Buzan.

Iroquois Gardens Club

Iroquois Gardens Apartments at the southwest corner of Park Road and New Cut Road was once the site of Iroquois Gardens Club. The nightclub was built in the late 1930s. N.L. Neafus was the manager in 1937 and 1938. W.E. Snider was proprietor in 1941. By 1951 Stanley C. McDonald and his wife Mildred "Mimi" McDonald were the owners. They continued to run the club until it closed.

Long time resident of the area, Mr. Al Stogner, described the building as a large, wood frame building that faced New Cut Road. When you entered the dining room the bandstand was to the left with a dance floor in the center of the room. The tables circled the dance floor from the right side of the door to the bandstand. Mr. Stogner recalled that "after you danced you could go up and shake the band leader's hand". Most people remember the outside garden area. There was a covered bandstand and dance floor area with tables under the trees. It was a wonderful place to spend a summer evening.

Vintage postcard is courtesy of Mort Childress.

Mrs. Betty Scott remembers working in the kitchen. She said it was located on the ground floor in back. Waiters came in and out the back door to the garden area. The Band and Dance floor were above the kitchen. She remembers an apartment above that where Mr. and Mrs. Snider lived. She tells of being there the night Glenn Miller played. Everyone wanted to hear him.

Mr. M. E. (Red) Smith remembers going to the club in 1953 or 1954. Their neighbors were a couple that did a dance/comedy routine and were working at Iroquois Gardens Club for a few weeks. Mr. Smith and his wife babysat the couple's little boy in the evenings while they were working. The couple gave Mr. and Mrs. Smith a free pass for one night at the end of their run. They went for the show and brought the couple's little boy with them. Mr. Smith remembers the inside dance floor was being used for the stage. At the end of the act, at a pre-arranged signal, Mr. And Mrs. Smith sent the little boy up to join his parents so they could introduce him to the audience.

Iroquois Gardens Club was known as a high class, expensive place with top name bands and performers, such as Benny Goodman, the Glenn Miller Band, Sammy Kaye, Tommy Dorsey, Glen Gray and the Casa Loma Orchestra, Paul Whiteman, Rudy Vallee, Clyde McCoy, Phyllis Diller, and Jayne Mansfield. Vaughn Monroe known for the songs "Racing With the Moon"(1941), "There, I've Said It Again"(1945), "Let It Snow, Let It Snow, Let It Snow"(1946), and "Ghost Riders In the Sky"(1949), performed there. Mrs. Mary Ellen Rateau Clements remembers him as being very good looking. She says her older sister Florence had a "crush" on him and even went out on a date with him.

Advertisement from a 1954 Iroquois Park Amphitheater Program is courtesy of Fred Banks.

It was a special place to go. Dr. and Mrs. Irvin (Eddie and Pat) Bronner recalled going there to celebrate some friends' wedding anniversaries. Mr. Fred Banks and his wife Patty remembered in the Spring of 1943 Patty's Louisville Girls High School's X-Lethean Club planned their Spring Formal Dance at Iroquois Gardens Club. There was a mix-up in the scheduling dates and Iroquois Gardens Club scheduled Ella Fitzgerald for the same night. When they discovered the mistake they honored their commitment to the girl's club. Ella Fitzgerald performed at their Spring Dance with the condition that the dance be open to the public.

Mr. Al Stogner and several others recalled that due to the expense they could not afford to go very often to the club. Instead they would park nearby, sit by the fence, and listen to the music. Mrs. Margie Simms Gibson remembers going as a teenager and parking the car on Park Road, listening to the music and dancing in the street.

Mrs. Mary Ellen Rateau Clements met her husband in the early 1940s. He was supposed to go into the service in two weeks and they decided to spend as much time as they could together. She remembers deciding to make a new dress for each night that they went out. When he told his mother how Mary Ellen had a new dress every night they went out, she told him, "you cannot afford that girl". He proved his mother wrong when he married her right after World War II ended. During the time they dated they went to Iroquois Gardens Club on several occasions. Mrs. Clements remembers the beautiful outside lighting. Her brother, Charley, took her to his Manual High School Prom at Iroquois Gardens around 1937. She said bands would often play for 3 to 4 weeks and then move on and someone else would come.

Photograph of Iroquois Gardens Club, outdoor bandstand and dance floor used with the permission of the University of Louisville Photographic Archives.

Mrs. Bertha Goss shared the following story with her granddaughter, Stefanie Buzan. Mrs. Goss was part of a group of 8-10 couples that frequented Iroquois Gardens on the weekends. "You did not go out of the house unless you were in your best clothes. I always wore a dress and Ray always had on a jacket and a tie", she recalled. One particular evening the group was indulging in cocktails and listening to the band in the outdoor garden at the club. At some point the men and women had a disagreement. Soon after this the husbands decided to relocate to a different table. When the next round of drinks arrived the women were determined not to reconcile with their husband over the price of a bar tab. Instead they pooled their money and not only paid the bill, but managed a thirty cent tip for the server. They were so pleased that they did not need their husbands to come to their aid that they began to laugh and cut up. As they finished their cocktails their laughter grew louder, prompting the Iroquois Gardens management to invite them to leave the premises. The women agreed to leave but, to the manager's surprise, they began climbing over the garden wall rather than exiting through the door. Since it was all in good fun, the husbands got up and followed their wives over the wall.

It was in 1964 that the McDonalds first sought rezoning of the club so that apartments could be built. The Iroquois Civic Club campaigned against the rezoning. In 1968 the City Planning Commission approved the building of apartments. Today just the name of the club remains in the name of the apartments that took its place. But the club continues to exist in the memories of so many Louisville residents that enjoyed a night of music and dancing under the stars.

Photograph of an ad from a 1942 Iroquois Amphitheater program is courtesy of the Iroquois Amphitheater Association.

CHAPTER 5

The Schools

Kenwood and Auburndale Elementary Schools

Although they are currently two separate schools, these schools share the same history. There have been many schools in the Kenwood Hill area before Kenwood and Auburndale. The earliest one may have been Steedley School in 1868. It was located on Strawberry Lane near Old Third Street Road. In 1870 it was relocated to East Strawberry Lane. It changed again in 1878 to a two room log school on Old Third Street Road. In 1887 a panel board school was erected near Iroquois Gardens on New Cut Road. This school was named Findley after the former owner of the land.

In a paper for her 1942 class at the University of Louisville, Mrs. Esther Lillian Preston Perkins tells that it was often difficult to find teachers for these early schools. The older boys of the neighborhood often proved difficult to handle by young teachers who had just graduated. One year when Miss Sarah Davis arrived about two weeks before school started the school trustee, Mr. Helwig, was not sure she could handle the boys. They agreed that she would teach for one month on trial. He could pay her off at that time if she proved unsatisfactory. She ended up teaching for five years until she got married. She was tall, (almost 6 feet), slender and about 30 years old. She is said to have whipped them if they did not do the right thing, read the bible every morning, and if they committed a wrong, she wrote the commandment they'd broken on the blackboard.

Early school located on New Cut Road, photograph is courtesy of Lillian Perkins and the University of Louisville Photographic Archives.

Kenwood School located at Strawberry Lane and Old Third Street Road, 1908, photograph is courtesy of Lillian Perkins and the University of Louisville Photographic Archives.

In 1897 the first school to be named Kenwood was erected at Old Third Street Road and Strawberry Lane. It boasted the first lunchroom, a basement with a furnace, and additional playground. It also created an organization which later became the first P.T.A. in Jefferson County. Mrs. Sam Stone Bush was the first president. All this came about through the efforts of Mr. Nicholas Finzer, a trustee. Mr. Finzer's hard work and dreams for an even better school were realized in 1913 when four acres of land on Palatka Road near Old Third Street Road was purchased from Mr. Sam Stone Bush and Mr. Gheens.

Construction on this new school was completed in 1916. It was a modern brick building with 3 classrooms, an auditorium and basement. The school population grew and so did the school. There were additions to the building in 1920 and 1932, more classrooms, an auditorium, and spiral fire escapes. In 1924 the name was changed to Auburndale because of a resemblance to Auburndale, Florida . In 1928 septic tank toilets replaced the old pit out houses. In 1929 a two room portable classroom was added. In 1934 another two rooms were built to the right of the other one with toilets in between as a connection. Around 1927 the first bus to serve the school was purchased due to the consolidation of several one room schools.

Photograph of Auburndale Elementary School, circa 1960, is courtesy of Jefferson County Public Schools.

One of the school's students, Mrs. Esther Lillian Preston Perkins remembers entering Auburndale School in 1927. She recalls that there were no classrooms in the basement at that time. There were five classrooms on the first floor and two on the second floor with a stage in the middle. The auditorium was to the front of the building with a water fountain and steps at the very front of the building. The lunchroom was in the basement. At one time the janitor lived in an apartment on the north end of the school, adjoining the kitchen. The restrooms were chemical tanks. The sinks to wash your hands were in the basement, outside the lunchroom. Miss Bertha Trunnell was the principal.

Photograph of outdoor restrooms is courtesy of Margie (Simms) Gibson.

Mrs. Perkins' family lived on Eiler Avenue off Strawberry Lane. There were cattle grazing in the field across from their home. Telephone, electricity, and water hookups didn't arrive until around 1940-41, when the Louisville Naval Ordnance plant was built.

Mrs. Esther Lillian Preston Perkins returned to Auburndale School in 1943 as a teacher. Miss Trunnell was still the principal. The area was still very rural, full of farm land. She remembers having students as old as 14 or 15 in her fourth grade class. These students had attended school very erratically and often did not finish a school year. They would have to complete it when they returned the next year. She taught her fourth graders on the stage the first two years due to overcrowding. She remembers teaching sixth grade one year and having 42 students. She also taught fourth grade two years in the same classroom where she had been a fourth grader. She tells of the school newspaper "The Auburndale Bugler". It was started about 1930 and was still being published in 1947. The students wrote articles about school events. "Ads" from neighboring churches and businesses were included in the paper.

Auburndale had a very strong health program. They won a silver cup in the 1930-31 school year for "attaining the highest standard in the achievement of good health". In 1937 a Health School was started and continued in operation for three years with Miss Walz as the teacher. The Courier Journal in December 1941 reports that the students put on a program which was an animated Christmas Seal. The students also sold bangle pins, small red double barred crosses, the international symbol for the fight against tuberculosis. This was to increase awareness of the disease and how to help prevent it.

Photograph of Auburndale School and school bus with the bus driver's (Walter Schroerlucke) son by the bus door and Imogene Middleton Smith entering the bus is courtesy of Rusty Cummings of Auburndale Auto.

Photograph of Nanette Horsley, in costume for the Auburndale School's Mountain Laurel Festival, standing by the portable classrooms is courtesy of Beverly Wheatley.

In the late 1940s Mrs. Sonja Gordon remembers Helen Keller paid a visit to Auburndale School. She said that being a young child she was just about as impressed with the seeing-eye dog as with Miss Keller. She did recall that Helen Keller told them to overcome obstacles and not to limit yourself. She said that you have a mind and should use it.

JEFFERSON COUNTY PUBLIC SCHOOLS

Auburndale School

Report of_____ of the *fifth* Grade

For the Year 19*23*-19*24* Age *12* Health_____ Average Weight *80*

B - 95 - 110
74 - 88 - 94
9 - 80 - 87
5 - 74 - 79
P - 53 - 69
4 - 0 - 54

	Days Present	Days Absent	Times Tardy	Health	Actual Weight	Deportment	Reading	Penmanship	Spelling	Language	Grammar	Geography	History	Arithmetic	Civil Government	Physiology	Drawing	Nature Studies	Agriculture	Physical Training	PARENTS OR GUARDIAN'S SIGNATURE
SEPTEMBER	14	0			80	a	4	44	6		E	4	9	74+		V8				1	
OCTOBER	20	0				E	4	74	89		V9	84	7	94		V9				2	
NOVEMBER	18		0			E	9	9	79		9	9	7	9		84				3	
DECEMBER	7	1	0			E9	9	9	F		F	F	P	F		F F				4	
JANUARY	14	6	0		87	6	79	9	6		V9	9	F	E		9	V8				5	
FEBRUARY	18	2	0			E	V9	9	19		E	V9	9	E		V9	V9				6	
MARCH	15	5	0			E	V9	V9	E		V9	19	79	E			9				7	
APRIL	18	0	0			E	19	19	E		79	19		E		V9				8	
MAY	20	0	0		91	E	19	19	E		19	V9		E						9	
JUNE																				10	
FOR YEAR																					

Recommended for Promotion to *6th* Grade ORVILLE J. STIVERS, Supt.
Recommended for Trial in_____ Grade *Willie Minor Miller* Teacher

NOTE—This report is sent to parents for the purpose of keeping them informed of the punctuality and regularity in attendance and standing in scholarship of the pupil and is to be taken as the standard for promotion. The figures in the column marked "For Year" will be those upon which promotion is made.

Photograph of a 1924 report card is courtesy of Jefferson County Public Schools.

World War II brought rapid development to the area. In 1954 Auburndale had a peak enrollment of over 700 students. To relieve the over-crowding another school, Kenwood Elementary, on Bruce Avenue was constructed. When Kenwood Elementary opened in 1955, Miss Trunnell, the Auburndale principal, and most of her teaching staff transferred to the new Kenwood School. In 1969 the current Auburndale Elementary was built on New Cut Road. In 1970 the old Auburndale School was destroyed by fire. One resident recalls the children saying "Auburndale School, all burned down". The site is now Auburndale Park.

Both Kenwood and Auburndale Elementary Schools grew out of the heritage of those other schools. Both continue to serve the community. In 1995 Kenwood Elementary paid tribute to the history of South Louisville in a 3-panel tile mosaic, 8 feet wide and 12 feet tall. Artist Licia Priest from the Visual Arts Association worked with 87 fifth graders and 96 primary students to create it. It depicts the neighborhood and the school's place in it. It illustrates Churchill Downs, Iroquois Park and scenes of student life at Kenwood.

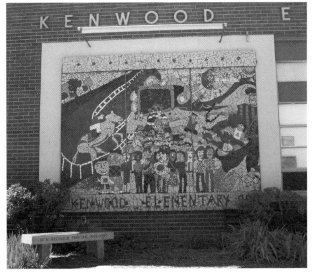

Photograph of the Kenwood Elementary mosaic, April 2006, is courtesy of Stefanie Buzan.

Many residents of the area shared their memories of the old Auburndale Elementary School on Palatka. It was the main elementary school for the area for 53 years. The most common memory was of the fire escape. It was a slide within a silo. Many remembered Fall Festivals where they sold tickets to ride down it. Mr. George Pierson remembers that about once a month a class would be chosen to take burlap bags and slide down the fire escape in order to polish it. Vickie Doherty Martin remembered moving to the area

and the school in 1953. She was in the fourth grade. She remembers the outdoor plumbing and that in the sixth grade indoor plumbing was finally installed. Vickie Martin also tells that in the fifth and sixth grades popcorn was delivered in large metal garbage cans and if you finished your work early you could help bag the popcorn in small bags to sell at the end of the school day. One year the money was used to buy shades for the classroom windows.

Both Auburndale School Fire Safety photographs, with the infamous fire escape, are courtesy of Lorretta Walker.

Vickie Martin, (and many others), remember Miss Bertha Trunnell. She was the principal from 1927-1955. She was also the first principal of the new Kenwood Elementary School from 1955 until 1967, the year she retired. That same year the Board of Education honored her dedication and commitment to education by naming the new school on St. Andrews Church Road the Bertha Trunnell Elementary School.

So many people have wonderful memories of the old Auburndale School, the building, the staffs, the students, and the activities. Perhaps Vickie Doherty Martin put it best though, "The best thing that came from the old Auburndale School is my friendship with Nancy Hill McGlaun which has been going on for over 50 years." What a treasure our elementary school years gave us in the friendships we had and sometimes still have. No wonder the memories of those years live on in our hearts.

Photograph of the Rateau children Earl, Florence and Charles, circa the late 1920s, dressed for a play at Auburndale school is courtesy of Mary Ellen Rateau Clements.

Photograph believed to be of one of the early Auburndale/Kenwood schools is courtesy of Jefferson County Public Schools.

Bertha Trunnell

The stories of Auburndale and Kenwood Elementary Schools cannot be told without mention of Miss Bertha Trunnell. Miss Trunnell was born in Bullitt County, Kentucky, on February 13, 1897. She graduated from Shepherdsville High School in May of 1916. From this time on she dedicated her entire life to teaching.

Miss Trunnell's first teaching assignment was in a one-room school in Bullitt County in 1916. She taught during school months and attended Western Kentucky State Normal School in the summers until she received her Bachelor of Art degree in 1931. She received her Master of Education Degree in 1949 from the University of Louisville.

In 1924 Miss Trunnell came to Auburndale Elementary as a teacher. She served as a teacher until 1927. She then became a teaching principal until 1945 and then assumed the position of full time principal until 1955. She spent 30 years at Auburndale. Mrs. Esther Lillian Preston Perkins, a student and later a teacher at Auburndale remembers that Miss Trunnell always came to school. She remembers that even when Miss Trunnell was sick and had very little voice she would come to school. Miss Trunnell was so dedicated to the children. When Auburndale Elementary became overcrowded, Kenwood Elementary was built to relieve the overcrowding. Miss Trunnell was selected as the first principal in 1955. On May 16, 1955 the Iroquois Civic Club put on a program to honor Miss Trunnell for her years of service at Auburndale. The program was a take off on the "This Is Your Life" television program. Many of Miss Trunnell's family, friends, and fellow educators attended. Miss Trunnell commented that when she came to Auburndale the school was called the Kenwood School, "and it's like starting a part of my life over again" to go to the new Kenwood School.

Miss Bertha Trunnell receiving a fire safety award from the fire marshal and R.K. Walker. Photograph is courtesy of Lorretta Walker.

Miss Trunnell served as principal at Kenwood Elementary for twelve years until she retired in June of 1967. Upon retirement she said that she planned a trip to Hawaii and would spend time with friends, work in her garden and sleep later in the mornings. The P.T.A. members presented her with a hand-stitched needlepoint purse with a check inside for a mink stole. But the highest honor was to come from the Jefferson County school Board. In the fall of that same year, 1967, a new elementary school was to open on St. Andrews Church Road. The Jefferson County Board of Education named the school Bertha Trunnell Elementary in her honor, citing her life-long dedication to the educational profession. Miss Trunnell stated in a letter to the Board of Education that she considered this the highest of honors and that she had never dreamed that anything like that would happen to her.

Miss Trunnell died at the age of 84 in 1981. To this day so many people remember Miss Trunnell fondly. Perhaps that's the best tribute of all.

Rutherford Elementary School

At the northwest corner of Southland Boulevard and 3rd Street sits the imposing structure of Rutherford Elementary School. It was named for Sallie B. Rutherford who for 57 years served the Louisville Public Schools as a teacher, principal, and district superintendent. Construction of the school began in 1950. Rutherford opened in September of 1951 with an enrollment of 862 students. The school was dedicated in March of 1952. Hazelwood Elementary School on Bluegrass Avenue opened the same year. These two South End schools were the first elementary schools in either the city or county to have a separate room set aside for a library. Both schools have gymnasiums large enough to accommodate basketball games. Rutherford was designed to have 30 classrooms and was built so that the building faces toward Iroquois Park.

Photograph of the front cover of the Rutherford Dedication Brochure is courtesy of Jefferson County Public Schools.

It has a 15 acre playground surrounding the building. According to the Dedication Brochure a second grade child described the construction of the playground as such, "First they put down the rocks,
Next they put in the tar.
Then it was covered with gravel.
The last thing was asphalt.
They rolled it smooth.
Next it will be covered with children."
For 55 years the playground has been covered with children.

Photograph of the Rutherford Elementary School playground in 1951 with Iroquois Park in the background is courtesy of Jefferson County Public Schools.

When the school opened Miss Helen Weaver was the first principal with the following staff of 27 teachers.

Teacher	Grade	Teacher	Grade	Teacher	Grade
Miss Rose Bere	6	Mrs. Anna Morton	3	Mrs. Rose Gressman	1
Mr. Thomas Whitfield	6	Miss Edith Frabue	3	Miss Mildred Bloom	1
Mrs. Dorothy Harris	5	Mrs. Freida Freeman	3	Mrs. Judy Pelham	1
Mrs. Dorothy Schultz	5	Miss Mary Caden	3	Mrs. Patricia Shaw	1
Mrs. Ida Dunbar	5	Miss Estelle Johnson	3	Mrs. Laverne Larrabee	K
Miss Edith Elliot	4	Mrs. Alice Watts	2	Miss Willie H. Slaby	K
Mrs. Susan Carter	4	Mrs. Margaret Marshall	2	Mrs. Elizabeth Morris	K
Mrs. Rosalie Jones	4	Mrs. Ethel Threlkeld	2	Mrs. Virginia Long	K
Miss Norma Brown	4	Mrs. Jeanette Thomas	2	Miss Pearl Williams	K

Faculty

STANDING: LEFT TO RIGHT. Mrs. Rosalee Jones, Edith Elliott, Willie Howard Slaby, Mrs. Ida Dunbar, Rose Bere, Mrs. Elizabeth Morris, Mrs. Freida Freeman, Norma Brown, Mrs. Anna Morton, Pearl Williams, Mrs. Elizabeth Bogart, Mrs. Rose Gressman, Mrs. Virginia Long, Mrs. Susan Carter, Mrs. Henrietta Schneider.

SEATED: LEFT TO RIGHT. Mrs. Jeanette Thomas, Mrs. Margaret Marshall, Mrs. Martha Mink, Mrs. Dorothy Schultz, Mrs. Patricia Shaw, Mildred Bloom, Mrs. Catherine Pelham, Helen Weaver, Edith Ross Trabue, Mrs. Estelle Johnson, Mary Caden, Mrs. LaVerne Larrabee, Mrs. Dorothy Harris, Mrs. Alice Watts, Mrs. Ethel Threlkeld.

Photograph of the 1951 Rutherford elementary staff is courtesy of Jefferson County Public Schools.

On the first day of school there were no sidewalks completed, not even temporary ones. This left mud for the students to navigate through to get to the building. When Lisa King (then 8 years old) got stuck, Janitor Earl Clark had to rush out to get her free from the muck. Some students came prepared and wore boots. "Mud Trim" became the style of the day.

Rutherford Elementary School has changed very little over the years. The trees are much larger now and the sidewalks prevent some of the mud from the children's shoes. Many children (and staff), have passed through those doors. Today the school continues to help educate the young children of the neighborhood.

Photograph of Rutherford Elementary, May 2006, is courtesy of Stefanie Buzan.

Gottschalk Junior High School, Rubado Elementary

The buildings we know today as Iroquois High School and Iroquois Middle School did not start with these names. They were both built as different schools for different purposes than what they now serve. Iroquois High School was once Gottschalk Junior High School and Iroquois Middle School was Rubado Elementary School.

Photographs of Rubado Elementary School, 1956, (now Iroquois Middle School), are courtesy of Jefferson County Public Schools.

In 1956 Rubado Elementary School opened at 5650 Southern Parkway. The school was named for Dr. Clarence A. Rubado, the Assistant Superintendent in charge of elementary education for the Louisville Public Schools for 25 years. It remained an elementary school until 1965 when it became Gottschalk Junior High School.

Gottschalk Junior High School, for grades 7, 8, and 9, was first housed in the building that is now Iroquois High School at 4615 Taylor Boulevard. Gottschalk Junior High School was named for Mr. Edward Gottschalk who served for 24 years as a member of the Louisville Board of Education. He is credited with working toward the passage of laws providing free textbooks for school children in Kentucky. Gottschalk Junior High School opened in 1956, the same time as Rubado Elementary. Both schools were designed to be modern in every detail. Rubado boasted of its all purpose room serving as lunchroom, auditorium and play space. Gottschalk had special rooms for shop, art, music and household arts. Gottschalk also had a communication center which contained its own AM-FM radio, phonograph, and tape recorder that permitted broadcasts from the office, the auditorium, or any classroom, to any other one, or group of rooms, in the building. This in-house intercom system was new technology for the time. All the classrooms had a forced-air ventilator to provide clean, fresh air at the correct temperature.

The schools were built on a 34 acre plot of land with adjoining playgrounds. The original plan was for a third building, a high school, to be built adjoining Gottschalk Junior High School, sharing some of the facilities. This third building was never constructed.

The residents of the South End of Louisville had pressed for a high school in the area since the early 1950s. DuPont Manual High School had become severely overcrowded, so in October of 1964 the decision was made to establish the high school in the Gottschalk Junior High School Building. Rubado Elementary became a transitional junior high for grade 7 that year and the name was changed to Gottschalk Junior High School. Iroquois High School opened in the fall of 1965 with grades 8, 9, and 10. These students would move on to become grades 10, 11, and 12 in two year's time. June of 1968 saw the first graduates of Iroquois High School.

Photograph of Gottschalk Junior High School, (now Iroquois High School), circa 1956, is courtesy of Jefferson County Public Schools.

The Iroquois High School district was large and included a "fringe area" served by the then county schools. Kenwood Hill was part of this fringe area. The students could elect to attend Southern High School in the county system or Iroquois. The county system paid tuition for those who chose Iroquois.

In 1973 Gottschalk Junior High School was renamed Iroquois Junior High School at the request of the students, neighborhood board and community. In 1976 grade 9 was moved from Iroquois Junior High to Iroquois High School. The high school and junior high school temporarily merged to handle the increase in enrollment. The junior high was known as Building B and the high school as Building A. In 1977 when a new addition to the high school was completed the schools separated again. Building B reopened as Iroquois Middle School, with grades 6, 7, and 8 and Iroquois High School had grades 9, 10, 11, and 12.

Iroquois High School became a Magnet Career Academy in the 1990s. It provides a Construction Technology Program which offers a combination of technical and academic programs. It has an award winning Navy JROTC program and participates in the National Academy of Finance. It offers both Advance and Honors programs.

Both Iroquois High School and Iroquois Middle school have a rich history of educating the youth of the area. The school buildings have been here for 50 years. They continue today to be an important part of the community.

Photograph of Iroquois High School, May 2006, is courtesy of Rosemary McCandless.

DeSales Catholic High School

A prominent landmark to the neighborhood is DeSales High School at 425 Kenwood Drive. The school sits on property that was once the Delph family farm. When the farm was put up for sale Mr. Gus Bronner, who lived across Kenwood Drive, purchased the property. He planned to divide the land into lots for houses. He sold the first lot to Mr. Ratterman. At this time the Archdiocese approached Mr. Bronner about selling the property to them for a new high school. Archbishop John A. Flourish saw the need for a boy's Catholic high school in the fast growing and heavily Catholic South End of Louisville. There were no Catholic high schools in the area. As Dr. Irvin (Eddie) Bronner tells it, his dad, Mr. Gus Bronner, was delighted to sell the property to the Archdiocese and Mr. Ratterman, being of a good Catholic family, also sold the Archdiocese the lot he had purchased. And so the stage was set for the new high school to be built.

Photograph of DeSales High School construction, 1956, are from the 1957 DeSales High School Freshman Yearbook.

Archbishop Flourish approached the Carmelite Order to staff the new school. It was named for Saint Francis DeSales who is considered a patron of writers and journalists. DeSales High School first opened on September 10, 1956 with a class of 130 freshmen boys. Father Jude Cattelona was the first principal. Three other priests, Fathers Linus Crowley, Ronan Lee, and Casmir Zelinski, and Mr. D. Crocetti joined Father Jude as the first teaching staff. Tuition was $50.00 the first year. It increased to $75.00 the year the first class graduated.

When the school opened that September the construction was not complete. The wing facing Kenwood was completed, minus the monastery and chapel. The wing that faces Laughlin Avenue and has the cafeteria was not built until later that year. The school only had freshmen that first year so there were some unused classrooms available for alternative uses. Since there was no cafeteria, the students would bring their lunches and eat in a couple of the unused classrooms. Since the monastery was not completed, some of the classrooms on the unused second floor were designated for the priests to live in.

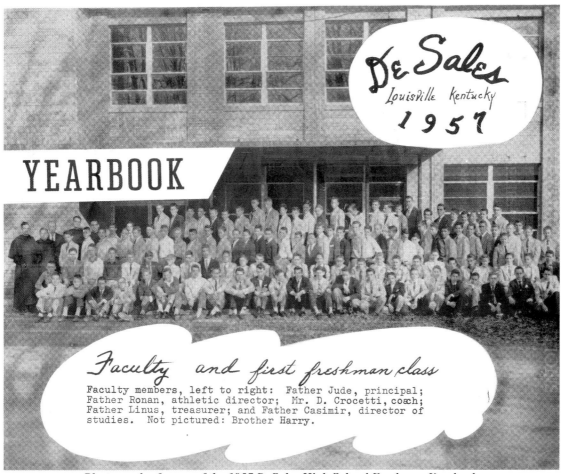

Photograph of cover of the 1957 DeSales High School Freshman Yearbook.

Mr. Gary Burge, Mr. Bob Coke and Mr. Bob West were part of that first freshman class. They told of a fundraiser the school had that first year. They raffled off chances of a green Nash Metropolitan car. The car was very small, almost like a midget car. It was so little that at the close of school each day one of the priests would drive it through the front doors and park it in the hallway overnight.

Mr. David Cecil came to DeSales as a sophomore the second year the school was open. He tells of the smoking ban at school. No smoking within one block of school. One of the students, Ervie Sipes decided to run for class president on the platform that he would get them a "smoking room" if elected. Although everyone knew that would never happen, Ervie Sipes was elected. Everyone must have liked his originality.

Mr. Rich Schulten joined the first graduating class his junior year. He felt it was different from the other high schools since it was a South End school. The students all came from the area and knew each other. It was like a neighborhood school. He shared his memory of the Fish Fry held every Friday as a fundraiser. The parents volunteered to cook and serve. Afterwards the students had a Teen Club. He also recalled that the mothers would volunteer to help in the cafeteria to keep expenses down. Some mothers continued to work there even after their sons had graduated.

On May 29, 1960, 85 young men were the first graduates of the school. The ceremony took place in the Iroquois Park Amphitheater. Over 5,000 young men have attended DeSales since it started. It was one of the first high schools in the Louisville area to equip itself with computers and require a computer literacy course. Today DeSales is a self-sufficient Archdiocesan-sponsored Catholic high school. They continue the tradition started in 1956 of providing a quality, Catholic education in a small, all-male environment. Perhaps one of the nicest things to be said about the school was from one of those early graduates. He felt it was a good school to go to, and that his closest friends today are several of those classmates from DeSales.

Photographs of DeSales High School, May 2006 are courtesy of Rosemary McCandless.

CHAPTER 6

The Churches

St. Mark's Lutheran Church ❖ St. Thomas More Catholic Church and School
Our Lady of Mount Carmel Catholic Church and School
Epiphany Methodist Church ❖ Kenwood Baptist Church
Auburndale Baptist Church ❖ Lynn Acres Baptist Church
Kenwood Heights Christian Church ❖ Our Lady of La-Vang Statue

St. Mark Lutheran Church

St. Mark Lutheran Church on Southside Drive has a wonderfully rich history tracing back to the Little Loomhouse's Esta Cabin. This, the first of three cabins, was built in 1870. In 1907, Mary Wulff, a writer and artist, bought the cabin. An early Sunday School Class held in this cabin led to the founding of St. Mark Lutheran Church. In 1911 a building was erected on land donated by Mr. Charles E. Gheens. Mrs. Mary Wulff organized a Sunday School with Mrs. Nicholas Finzer and Mrs. Lena Gailbraith as the two teachers and Mr. McNair as superintendent. The church originally was non-denominational and was known as "Christian Union Church" or "Gheens' Mission". It was supplied by students from both the Louisville Presbyterian Seminary and the Southern Baptist Seminary. In November of 1919 they decided to become affiliated with the Lutheran Church. St. Mark Lutheran Church was organized in March of 1920. The Reverend S.W. Powell was the first regular pastor for the church.

Photograph of original church, (now a daycare), and parsonage
is courtesy of St. Mark's Lutheran Church.

The congregation began making several major improvements to the church property. In 1928 members and friends excavated and constructed a basement for the church to provide more space for the Sunday School. A memorial window was placed above the altar by Mr. and Mrs. Nicholas Finzer and their four sons in 1934. The brick parsonage was built next door to the church in 1937 on land provided again by Mr. Gheens. The land was cleared of the trees by then Pastor Alfred G. Belles and the men and boys of the church.

Photograph of St. Mark's Lutheran Church stained glass
window, May 2006, is courtesy of Rosemary McCandless.

After World War II the South End of Louisville was booming. St. Mark Lutheran Church outgrew the original church. Mr. Gheens donated a third piece of land and the current church was built. It was dedicated in 1953. The original church was remodeled for use as a parish house. Its bell, that rang every Sunday morning and on special occasions, is still remembered in the community.

Photographs of groundbreaking and construction of current church in 1953 are courtesy of St. Mark's Lutheran Church.

As St. Mark Lutheran Church approaches its 100th birthday it continues to be an important part of the community that it serves.

Photograph of St. Mark's Lutheran Church is courtesy of St. Mark's Lutheran Church.

St. Thomas More Catholic Church

Just prior to World War II Louisville's South End was expanding. In September of 1943 Archbishop John A. Floersh approved a new parish for the area. The site chosen for the church and school was the southeast corner of 3rd St. and Inverness Avenue. On February 22, 1944, the parish was named St. Thomas More. Father John P. Hannon served as the first pastor.

Four photographs of church and school construction are courtesy of St. Thomas More Catholic Church.

The original building was a two story, eight classroom, red brick, school and church combination. The building is still there today. The church was first used on July 6, 1944. The school opened its doors on September 11, 1944, with an enrollment of 204 students. Eight grades were taught by four Sisters of Charity of Nazareth. Sister Mary Clarence was the first principal.

The parish grew after World War II and the parish complex was expanded. The rectory was completed in 1949 and the convent in 1954 to house the twelve Sisters teaching in the school. The school was expanded at this time by six more classrooms, a new cafeteria and a gymnasium. The church was now too small for the large parish. In December of 1964 the cornerstone was laid for the current church. It was dedicated on January 20, 1965.

The territory of St. Thomas More began shrinking. There were four new parishes formed between 1944 and 1961 from the area once comprised by St. Thomas More: Saints Simon and Jude; St. John Vianney; St. Jerome in Fairdale; and Our Lady of Mount Carmel. In recent years there has been a decline in enrollment in the South End Catholic elementary schools. In August of 2005 St. Thomas More School joined Our Lady of Mount Carmel, Most Blessed Sacrament, and Saints Simon and Jude schools to create St. Nicholas Academy. It is housed at the old Mount Carmel and Saints Simon and Jude campuses.

Collage of photographs of the beginning of St. Thomas More Catholic Church and School is courtesy of St. Thomas More Catholic Church.

Photograph of St. Thomas More Catholic Church, May 2006, is courtesy of Rosemary McCandless.

Our Lady of Mount Carmel Catholic Church

Our Lady of Mount Carmel Catholic Church was established to meet the needs of the growing catholic population in the South End. St. Thomas More Catholic Church and school had already opened in 1944 at Third Street and Inverness Avenue. The large number of new homes being constructed in the area had swelled the population of this parish. In 1957 Archdiocesan authorities asked the Carmelite religious order to assume responsibility for the operation of a new parish. The first pastor was Fr. Luke Bresnahan, O.Carm. The site chosen for the church was a ball field, owned by the Fitzgibbon family, at the corner of New Cut Road and Old Third Street Road.

Construction photographs are courtesy of Our Lady of Mount Carmel Catholic Church.

The church began functioning immediately in 1957 with mass being offered at nearby Auburndale Elementary School on September 8. In 1940 Auburndale Baptist Church had also started by meeting at Auburndale Elementary. Construction of the building which houses the church and the current school cafeteria began in 1958. The school building was completed by September 28, 1959 and officially opened. The cafeteria became the site for masses until the church was completed. The dedication took place on November 13, 1960. The rectory was built in 1961. The pastor had been living at the DeSales High School monastery. A convent for the Dominican Sisters who staffed the school was completed in 1965. The Sisters had been living at Holy Rosary. The interior finishing, (painting and such), of the school, church, rectory, and convent was completed by members of the parish.

Construction photograph is courtesy of Our Lady of Mount Carmel Catholic Church.

During the construction of Our Lady of Mount Carmel, both St. Thomas More Parish and DeSales High School allowed the use of their facilities for parish events. The first parish picnic in July of 1958 was held on the grounds of St. Thomas More. Card parties and dances were held at DeSales. When Father Jude Cattelona, O.Carm, who had been the first principal of DeSales High School, came in 1969 to serve as pastor, he was indeed familiar to the parish. He remained as pastor until 1977.

The church and school continued to expand and be renovated. A large multi-purpose building with a gymnasium and several classrooms was constructed in 1978. A separate library/computer lab building was built in 1988. It has since been remodeled and converted for use as a Parish Adult Center. In 1994 the church was renovated. In the fall of 1998 the Gillen Education Center was completed. It houses a meeting room, school classrooms, a large library, and a state of the art computer lab.

In August of 2005 Our Lady of Mount Carmel School joined St. Thomas More, Most Blessed Sacrament, and Saints Simon and Jude schools to create St. Nicholas Academy. The school is housed in the former Mount Carmel and the Saints Simon and Jude campuses. They have grades 1 through 8.

Our Lady of Mount Carmel Catholic Church has grown from a membership of approximately 150 families in 1957 to over 1,250 today. In spite of its large size, the parishioners pride themselves on the family-like spirit that exists in their parish.

Photographs of Our Lady of Mount Carmel Catholic Church and St. Nicholas Academy, May 2006, are courtesy of Rosemary McCandless.

Epiphany Methodist Church

Epiphany Methodist Church, at 7032 Southside Drive, had its beginning as Kenwood United Methodist. On May 8, 1949, the church started with 15 members and R.E. Coleman as the first pastor. They opened their service at 9:45 that morning with the song "I'll Be a Sunbeam". In September of 1949 Reverend D.N. Crenshaw was appointed to the church. The original building with seating for 120 people was erected from two army barracks. It was a neat and attractive building with a small sign out front giving the name. The interior was ventilated and although it heated well in the winter, it was known not to be cooled adequately in the summer. The pews of the church came from an old church.

Photograph of the original Kenwood United Methodist Church is courtesy of
Epiphany Methodist Church.

During 1951-1952 the Annex was built on the back of the church for Sunday school rooms. The Parsonage was purchased March 3, 1952, and the garage behind it was enlarged to make a recreation room and additional Sunday school rooms if needed. At this time the playground behind the church was leased to the city for five years as a playground for the community.

The church was rapidly outgrowing the original building even with these additions. In July of 1956 the members broke ground for a new church. The consecration service and open house was on December 16, 1956. November 23, 1958 saw groundbreaking for the new educational building.

Photograph of Kenwood United Methodist Church is courtesy of Epiphany Methodist Church.

Kenwood United Methodist merged with Jones Memorial Methodist on September 2, 1990 to become Epiphany Methodist Church. The combined church soon realized a need for a larger building. Construction on the current building began in the summer of 1992. Through all the changes over the years, Epiphany Methodist has continued to be a vital part of the community.

Photograph of Epiphany Methodist Church, May 2006, is courtesy of Rosemary McCandless.

Kenwood Baptist Church

The 1940's saw great expansion in the South End of Louisville, especially after World War II. Kenwood Baptist Church was founded at this time as an outreach of Walnut Street Baptist Church. In the fall of 1943, Walnut Street Baptist Church sent Reverend Richard Bryant to survey the community to determine if there was an interest in forming a Baptist church in the area. He found several families expressing a desire for such a church and so Kenwood Baptist was started. They would meet over the next few years in the homes of various founding families, starting with the home of Mr. Gilbert King. Reverend Bryant would serve as the first pastor.

Photograph is courtesy of Bill King.

In early 1945 a building committee was elected. Walnut Street Baptist Church had contracted to purchase land at the corner of Third Street and Seneca Trail in August of 1944. It was decided that the church should be built in three stages. First a basement suitable for all activities would be constructed. A sanctuary could be added above at a later time. Finally, Sunday School rooms would be built. The Groundbreaking Service was held on April 29, 1945. The cornerstone was laid July 29 and on August 5 the building was occupied.

Photograph is courtesy of Bill King.

In 1949 the church was growing and had no place to put new Sunday School classes. Financially a new building was not possible. A frame duplex building on Ormsby Street was found that needed to be moved to make way for a new apartment building. It was sold to the church for $500.00 plus the cost of moving it. Mr. Bill King remembers the story of the building being moved up Third Street one weekend on a low-boy trailer. Unfortunately it was damaged in the moving and had to be completely remodeled including bricking over the exterior. It was used as the children and youth Sunday School and became known as "The Annex". The building was leased to South Louisville Community Ministries in 1991. It is still standing and is currently leased to the Evangelical Church Winning All (ECWA).

Photograph of former Kenwood Baptist Church Annex, April 2006, is courtesy of Stefanie Buzan.

By 1953 the church had outgrown its first building. It was decided that it would be too costly to build onto the original basement building due to deterioration. A new building consisting of a sanctuary, Sunday School rooms and church offices would be built along Third Street. This, the current building, was dedicated on December 9, 1956. In 1962 an extension was built to the rear of the chapel, the old basement building was then torn down and the lawn landscaped. Today Kenwood Baptist Church continues the vision of its founders - reaching out to the community it serves.

Photograph of Kenwood Baptist Church is courtesy of Irma Atwell.

Auburndale Baptist Church

There were very few churches in the Auburndale area in 1938. Families often had to travel to other neighborhoods to find the church of their choice. There were Baptist families here, but no Baptist church. During the summer of 1938 Beechmont Baptist Church sent Sunday School teachers to the area. Marie Rumsey Cook remembers having Sunday School lessons under the trees on Bruce Avenue.

In 1939 Carlisle Avenue Baptist Church held a tent revival in the Auburndale community. Families began having Sunday School classes in their homes. The number attending soon outgrew the homes and on July14, 1940, they began meeting at Auburndale Elementary School at the corner of Palatka Road and Third Street Road (Southside Drive). Reverend Leroy Parker was the first pastor.

In 1943, with the help of Carlisle Avenue Baptist Church, the first lot at the corner of Third Street Road and Bruce Avenue was purchased. The first building was a red brick half basement with an auditorium with seating for 150 people and six classrooms. In 1947 the parsonage was built. Auburndale Baptist Church was chartered in 1951 and no longer a mission of Carlisle Baptist Church. An adult Sunday School Department and Fellowship Hall was completed in 1955. A three story educational building was added in 1957. Construction on the current building began in 1959. On April 3, 1960, the congregation met to dedicate the sanctuary.

The Auburndale area has changed greatly from 1939, with businesses, shopping centers, apartment houses and subdivisions now surrounding the church. Through all the changes, the Auburndale Baptist Church has served and continues to serve the people of the Auburndale area.

Photograph of Auburndale Baptist Church, April 2006, is courtesy of Stefanie Buzan.

Lynn Acres Baptist Church

At 5007 Southside Drive is the impressive structure of Lynn Acres Baptist Church. In October of 2005 the church officially merged with Yorktown Baptist Church to become Grace Community Baptist Church. The new combined church is housed at the old Yorktown Baptist building. The Lynn Acres Baptist building currently houses a daycare.

Lynn Acres Baptist Church began in 1950 with early church members holding services in their homes. On January 14, 1951, the church moved into a store building on Evangeline Road and the next day, January 15, 1951, the church was organized and constituted as a church with 92 charter members. Brother Cort R. Flint was the first pastor. The church experienced rapid growth and in October, 1952, it moved into the auditorium of the recently completed Sallie B. Rutherford Elementary School at Third Street and Southland Boulevard.

Land was purchased from Mr. Leroy Highbaugh who was constructing numerous houses in the neighborhood. He was the builder of Lynn Acres Apartments (now Americana Apartments). He had no objection to the new church taking the name of Lynn Acres. He gave the church a good deal on the property and construction began. The church building on Southside Drive was completed in three phases. In November of 1952 they broke ground on the back part of the building. This section had Sunday School rooms and a large room that was used as a temporary sanctuary. The church dedicated this section and began using it on April 19, 1953. In November of 1961 the sanctuary was completed in front of the first section. The office wing was finished in August of 1965.

Although they are no longer housed in the old church building, they are still an important part of the neighborhood.

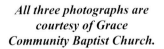
All three photographs are courtesy of Grace Community Baptist Church.

Kenwood Heights Christian Church

The Kenwood Christian Church was first conceived as a mission church of the Bennett Avenue Christian Church with the aid of the South Louisville Christian Church. These two churches jointly hired an evangelist to hold a revival-style meeting. This meeting produced 32 members for the new church. The church first met in basements and tents. Land was purchased at 6200 South Third Street in 1944. Phil Duncan was the minister. The first phase, a basement auditorium, was dedicated on December 17, 1944. On May 15, 1959, an auditorium and an educational plant were dedicated.

Two photographs of the original Kenwood Christian Church, April 2006, are courtesy of Stefanie Buzan.

In the fall of 1969 discussions began concerning the merger of Kenwood Christian Church with Flora Heights Christian Church at 1520 Dixie Highway. On November 16, 1969, the two churches first met together as one, becoming Kenwood Heights Christian Church. The church continued to experience steady growth. A new auditorium with a seating capacity of over 500 was built in 1976. In 1984 the Kenwood Preschool began. In October of 2004 the first phase of a building program was completed and the church moved to their current location at 5620 New Cut Road.

Photograph of the new Kenwood Heights Christian Church, April 2006, is courtesy of Stefanie Buzan.

Kenwood Heights Christian Church has undergone many changes since they first began. They continue to flourish and are proud to serve the South Louisville community.

Our Lady of La-Vang

As Second Street and Southside Drive become one, look toward St. John Vianney Catholic Church and you will see the 7 foot statue of Our Lady of La-Vang, standing upon a 13 foot long, seven headed dragon, blazing in brilliant white marble.

The statue is the result of the efforts of Anthony Chinh, associate pastor at St. John Vianney Catholic Church. Chinh realized that up to 15 percent of Louisville's Vietnamese residents are Catholic. He was on a quest to get Vietnamese parishioners involved in the church. Understanding that many of the Vietnamese residents did not feel at home, he sought to develop a shrine to Our Lady of La-Vang in an effort to reach out to them.

Our Lady of La-Vang is derived from Vietnamese history. At the end of the 18th century, Vietnamese Christians were fleeing persecution from the king; while in hiding, the lady appeared to them in a place called La-Vang. She comforted them by saying; "I will be with you." The dragon heads are to depict expression of visions in the Book of Revelation and Vietnamese mythology.

Le Pham, a local artist, designed the statue. Chinh traveled to Vietnam in search of a sculptor. At the end of a winding dirt road, he found Quan Phan. It took Quan Phan eight months to complete the statue. He asked only $7,000 for his work. The statue was shipped from Ho Chi Minh City, via boat in two pieces, the Madonna and the dragon. Once the statue arrived in Los Angeles, it boarded a train for Louisville. The entire trip took about a month.

Volunteers began preparing the site for the statue. The area was landscaped with thousands of colorful flowers and Japanese maples. The shrine includes plaques with Ave Maria in 12 languages. The Iroquois language is included. The outer ring of the shrine has street lamps, each flanked by protective gargoyles.

Photograph, 2006, is courtesy of Stefanie Buzan.

Our Lady of La-Vang is facing northwest, where many of the Vietnamese work. She greets them as they return to their homes each day. And appropriately, our Lady of La-Vang is facing toward Vietnam.

CHAPTER 7

The Businesses

Louisville Naval Ordnance ❖ Simms Corner ❖ Kenwood Drive-In ❖ Ken Bowl Lanes
Smith – Fitzgibbon Family, Auburndale Village Shopping Center
Phelp's Hardware ❖ Gordon's Corner ❖ Escher's Grocery ❖ Pony Heaven Farm
Iroquois Manor Shopping Center ❖ Douglas Park Race Course ❖ Thornberry's
Casey Jones Trains ❖ Colonel Walker Flag Company ❖ The First Doctors
Parkside Drive-In Restaurant ❖ Kenwood Fire Station

Louisville Naval Ordnance

One of the strongest influences in the development of the modern day South End was Louisville Naval Ordnance. Occupying ten blocks between Southside Drive and Strawberry Lane, the original site opened in 1941. Renamed Technology Park in 1996, when privatized by local government, the park consists of 142 acres with 84 buildings.

Photographs of the construction of Louisville Naval Ordnance are courtesy of the Naval Ordnance Retirees Association.

Louisville Naval Ordnance, a product of World War II, was responsible for the development and construction of some of the Navy's most high tech weapons. In its heyday, Naval Ordinance employed nearly 4,000 people.

Photographs of Louisville Naval Ordnance workers are courtesy of the Naval Ordnance Retirees Association.

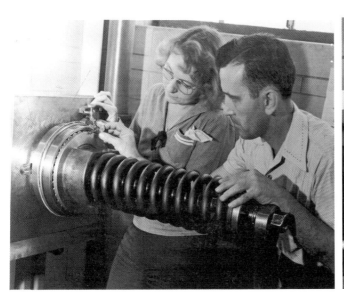

As a result of the vast number of Louisville Naval Ordnance employees, a housing boom resulted in close proximity, shaping the surrounding neighborhoods as they are today. The popular Highbaugh Homes that line the streets between Southside Drive and Third Street are indicative of the post World War II American Dream. The desirable floor plan had all of the amenities necessary for raising a family.

Louisville Naval Ordinance maintained a high standard as a good community citizen for its entire existence by providing annual 4th of July fireworks shows, free storage for local charities and cultural organizations as well as little league baseball.

Today, Technology Park is home to two the nation's largest defense contractors, United Defense and Raytheon Contractors. Supported by a group of on-site Navy engineers, Technology Park continues to service the Navy, repairing and manufacturing its large guns and missile systems.

NOSL Commanding Officers		
Name	**Rank**	**Years at NAVORDSTA**
K. M. McClaren	CDR, USN	Jul 1941 - Feb 1942
C. E. Brine	CDR, USN	Feb 1942 - Oct 1944
F. D. Kirtland	CAPT, USN	Oct 1944 - Dec 1944
R. M. Briggs	CDR, USN	Dec 1944 - Dec 1945
Clyde R. Robinson	CAPT, USN	Dec 1945 - Apr 1946
Omer A. Kneeland	CAPT, USN	Apr 1946 - May 1950
MC W. Wood	CAPT, USN	Jul 1950 - Sep 1953
R. A. Larkin	CAPT, USN	Sep 1953 - Jul 1955
H. N. Larson	CAPT, USN	Jul 1955 - Jun 1958
W. C. Butler, JR.	RADM, USN	Jun 1958 - Oct 1959
Robert L. Taylor	CAPT, USN	Oct 1959 - Jun 1961
William H. Fisher	CDR, USN (Acting)	Jul 1961 - Aug 1961
A. R. Faust	CAPT, USN	Aug 1961 - Nov 1963
R. L. Sattler	CAPT, USN	Nov 1963 - Jun 1968
H. R. Joy	CAPT, USN	Jun 1968 - Apr 1969
H. C. Anson	CAPT, USN (Acting)	Apr-69
P. H. McGann	CAPT, USN	Apr 1969 - Sep 1970
W. F. Hahnert, JR	CAPT, USN	Sep 1970 - Oct 1970
C. L. Scherrer	CAPT, USN	Oct 1970 - Jun 1972
W. C. Klemm	CAPT, USN	Jun 1972 - Jul 1975
W. C. Deal, JR	CDR, USN	Jul 1975 - Jul 1977
J. R. Haynes	CAPT, USN (Acting)	Jul 1977 - Aug 1977
H. M. Dejarnette	CAPT, USN	Aug 1977 - Jun 1980
T. C. Warren	CAPT, USN	Jun 1980 - Oct 1983
W. C. Long	CAPT, USN	Oct 1983 - May 1988
J. B. Brady	CAPT, USN	May 1988 - Jun 1991
R. W. Gilbert	CAPT, USN	Jun 1991 - Aug 1994
J. R. Cummings	CAPT, USN	Aug 1994 - Mar 1996
D. L. Porter	CDR, USN	Mar 1996 - Jul 1996
J. A. Fawbush JR.	CDR, USN	Jul-96

Simms Corner

The corner of Southside Drive and the National Turnpike, where the BB&T Bank is located today, was once home to a two story, brick structure with a large porch spreading across the front and wrapping down the south side of the building. There were benches on the porch and under the large Sycamore trees and people loved to sit on them and talk. This building bore a sign that simply read Simms Corner. It was built sometime around 1936.

Simms Corner photograph is courtesy of Rusty Cummings of Auburndale Auto.

The Simms Brothers in front of Simms Corner photograph courtesy of Margie (Simms) Gibson.

Simms Corner housed a bar on one side, a restaurant on the other side and the Simms Family above. Both the restaurant and the bar were owned and operated by Leonard "Len" and Margaret Simms. It is not common knowledge but prior to 1936, Simms Corner was a white, frame building with the same layout. The frame building was destroyed by a fire in 1936. Len Simms broke his ankle when he jumped from a second floor window to escape the flames. After the fire, the Simms rebuilt with the brick structure and continued to operate Simms Corner in the same location for another 20 years.

John, Darrell and Lenn Simms- interior shot of the original Simms Corner frame structure, prior to its destruction by fire. Photograph is courtesy of Margie (Simms) Gibson.

Fire destruction of the original Simms Corner, photograph courtesy of Margie (Simms) Gibson.

The restaurant was known for Margaret's delicious fish and pies. The pie crust was especially popular. Len and Margaret's daughter, Margie Gibson, recalled that her mother really did not use recipes, "just a little bit of this and a little bit of that, she usually mixed enough ingredients to make five pies at once."

The bar sold liquor by the drink and stocked the popular beers of the time, Oertels 92, Fehrs, Sterling and Falls City. Johnny and Bernice Baker were long time employees at Simms Corner. Johnny helped out in the bar while his wife helped out in the kitchen.

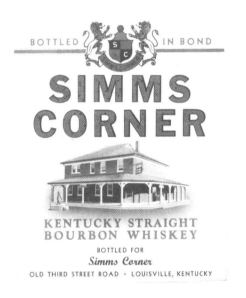

Top: Simms Corner custom bourbon label courtesy of Pete Gibson. Right: Officer Tom Simms in front of Simms Corner photograph courtesy of Margie (Simms) Gibson.

Left: Photograph of the exterior of Simms Corner neighboring grocery store on National Turnpike is courtesy of Margie (Simms) Gibson.

Simms Garage photograph is courtesy of Rusty Cummings, Auburndale Auto Parts.

Simms Corner was considered a little Louisville landmark of a sort. There was a mile marker sign in the shape of an arrow as far south as Dixie Highway, near Valley High School. The arrow pointed east towards Simms Corner.

The sign indicated Simms Corner was the building at the corner of Southside Drive and National Turnpike but it was much more than that. In addition to the building, the Simms family owned the adjoining ball field and concession stand, a separate grocery store and Len's brother, Clarence, owned Simms Garage across the street.

Photograph of the interior of grocery is courtesy of Margie (Simms) Gibson.

The ball field was surrounded by large Sycamore trees and hosted both men's and women's tournaments. Eventually, the Kenwood Drive-In would back up to the ball field. A well traveled path from the ball field to the drive-in would develop over time.

After Len's death in 1952 Margaret continued to run the Corner on her own. It became increasingly difficult so she decided to lease the property. In 1978 Margaret sold the land and the building to the Bank of Louisville, which today is known as BB&T Bank. According to Brad Wilson, at the time the Bank of Louisville was built, some of the neighborhood folks referred to it as the Simms Corner branch.

Interesting Fact: The benches that previously sat on the porch of Simms Corner, on which so many folks enjoyed passing their time, remain in the Simms Family. Today, they are sitting around the pool at Margie Gibson's son's house. Margie herself has the large, glass Planter's Peanut Jars that sat on the bar for so many years.

Photograph of John, Darrell and Len Simms behind the bar at Simms Corner is courtesy of Margie Simms Gibson.

The Kenwood Drive-In

Located at 7001 Southside Drive is a lone, remaining piece of a bygone era, the Kenwood Drive In. Construction of the Kenwood Drive-In was completed in June of 1949. It was built by William Porter. At the time of its birth it was one of 120 drive-ins in Kentucky - the sixth to be built in Louisville. Today, it is one of 17 remaining in the state, and the only one remaining in the City of Louisville.

The concept of a drive-in theater evolved when Richard Hollingshead had a desire to combine his two main interests, cars and movies. He mounted a 1928 Kodak projector to the hood of his car and took aim at a screen he nailed to a couple of trees in his back yard. He placed a radio behind the screen to enable sound. He first patented his unique idea on May 16, 1933 and opened the first drive-in theater on Tuesday, June 6, 1933 in Camden, New Jersey. The cost was 25 cents for the car and an additional 25 cents per person.

Photograph of the Simms Family Dog with the Kenwood Drive-In in the distance is courtesy of Margie (Simms) Gibson, taken circa 1950.

Although the drive-in theater had been in existence since 1933, the idea of the drive-in did not peak until the 1950s. Allen C. Wallace, president of Kenwood Drive-In at the time of construction touted several features of the new outdoor theater, "the wall for the screen is 71 feet high and 72 feet wide and is able to withstand 100- mile an hour winds". More than 3000 bolts and 19 kegs of nails were used when building the wall. Additionally, the drive-in included hard wired speakers that were mounted on the side of the moviegoer's car for sound and the 36 acre ground had capacity to hold 800 cars. According to Wallace, at the time it was built, the cost was $100,000.

Folks who frequented the Kenwood in the late 1960's fondly remember a fun fireworks show over the course of the evening. Long time resident Diane Hoagland recalled a time when cars would line up all the way down Southside Drive to get into the drive-in.

Other drive-ins you might remember that were in close proximity to the Kenwood are:

Dixie Drive-In   **Skyway Drive-In**   **Valley Drive-In**
Parkway Drive-In   **Twilight Drive-In**   **Preston Drive-In**

In 2006, the Kenwood Drive-in is owned and operated by National Amusements and it is one of a kind. A modern day feature includes broadcast sound at 87.9 on the FM dial of the moviegoer's stereo. The Kenwood Drive-in's season runs May – September.

Vintage Kenwood Drive-In movie poster image is courtesy of
John Story and Drive-ins.com.

Ken Bowl Lanes
Contributed by Thelma Carter

February 25, 1962, the Courier-Journal announced construction started on million-dollar Ken Bowl Lanes, on Southside Drive. It was the first free standing building of its size devoted solely to bowling. The new 36 lane house opened in early August 1962, with a cocktail lounge and a snack bar. It has been an asset to the community for over forty years with a strong youth and senior citizens program, providing fun and entertainment for all ages.

Original architect's drawing of Ken Bowl, courtesy of Thelma Carter.

The building was designed by architect Peyton Davis and the general contractor was Harry Mathely. The original cocktail lounge was called The Moulin Rouge. It was described as Louisville's newest fashionable cocktail-entertainment lounge with beautiful French décor, Parisian atmosphere and entertainment. The lounge was later redecorated and is now called the Southside Lounge.

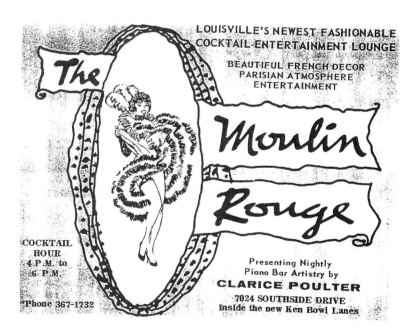

Advertisement for The Moulin Rouge is courtesy of Thelma Carter.

Over the years, Ken Bowl has had bowlers starting in leagues who are now bringing their children and grandchildren for recreation. The lanes are kept updated with computerized scoring and lane conditions. Each year for the past 19 years, Ken Bowl has offered a FREE DAY for kids in the community- free bowling, coke and hot dog, balloons and goodie bags for each child. There are as many as 500 children attending. The same is offered to Senior Citizens once a year.

Ken Bowl participates in community projects such as Crusade for Children and local fire department activities.

The Ken Bowl Lanes, Inc., and Dixie Bowl Lanes, Inc., are owned and operated by the Carter family- three generations and the fourth coming along. They take great pride in their business and their community.

Courtesy of Thelma Carter

The Smith-Fitzgibbon Family
Auburndale Village Shopping Center

In the late 1920s at the southwest corner of Old Third Street Road and New Cut Road there was a small grocery and gas station called Smith and Walker Grocery. Lillian Walker Smith owned about 22 acres where the Auburndale Village Shopping Center and Kroger Grocery Store are now. Her brother, Mr. C.J. Walker was her partner in the grocery. He was also the butcher for the store. An old log cabin was on the property located approximately where the Kroger stands today. During the Depression, in the 1930s, the cabin was rebuilt into a two story frame house by men who worked to earn food from the store for their family. Mrs. Smith kept a detailed record of the hours each man worked and how much food he had earned. Mrs. Smith lived in that house for a number of years.

Photographs of the log cabin of Mrs. Lillian Smith before remodeling are courtesy of Jim Fitzgibbon.

Photographs of Mrs. Lillian Smith's home after the cabin was rebuilt into a frame house are courtesy of Jim Fitzgibbon.

Mrs. Smith's daughter, Lillian Smith was married to Mr. Robert Fitzgibbon and they had three children, Robert, Jean, and James. Mr. and Mrs. Robert Fitzgibbon and their family lived with Mrs. Smith. Mr. Jim Fitzgibbon remembers growing up in his grandmother's house. It was a very rural area. On the east side of New Cut Road, right after the railroad tracks was a sheep farm owned by Mr. Probst. He also remembers that during World War II the chocolate Easter Bunnies and eggs were not available due to war shortages. Mr. Fitzgibbon's grandmother, (Mrs. Smith), and his mother, decorated candy bars to sell in the store for Easter by putting little icing birds and flowers on them. They wanted the children to still have special Easter candy. Mr. Jim Fitzgibbon tells that one of the services his grandmother offered was home delivery of the groceries. As a boy he found it fun to go along on these deliveries. Many residents of the area remember getting their groceries delivered from the store.

Mr. Robert Fitzgibbon was in business with Mr. "Boots" Siegel and they together owned Siegel's Feed and Hardware Store on Old Third Street Road (now Phelps' Hardware Store on Southside Drive). Mr. Fitzgibbon also built Auburndale Lumber Company on the east side of New Cut Road near the railroad tracks. Eventually the men decided to split the partnership. Mr. Siegel retained ownership of the Siegel Feed and Hardware Store. Mr. Robert Fitzgibbon also served as a Water Commissioner. He worked with Mr. Edward Jungbert, (another Water Commissioner), to get water service out to the Auburndale/Fairdale Community.

Photograph of Auburndale Feed and Lumber Company is courtesy of Jim Fitzgibbon.

In the early 1950s the family built a small strip of stores, facing New Cut Road by the grocery store. This strip of stores included Carter's Radio and TV Shop, Auburndale Drug Store (with a soda fountain), Gus Slaten's Barber Shop, and a beauty shop. In 1957 the Catholic Archdiocese of Louisville bought the southeast corner of New Cut Road and Southside Drive from the family in order to build a new church and establish a new parish, Our Lady of Mount Carmel. This corner had been a ball field for a number of years.

Strip mall, grocery and gas station, Sept. 1950. Photograph is courtesy of Jim Fitzgibbon.

In the 1960s the area was rapidly changing. The bus line had already started coming out to the Auburndale area in the early 1950s. After World War II the entire area was experiencing a building boom. New housing subdivisions were under construction all around them. The population was increasing and more stores were needed. In the mid 1960s the family grocery and the other small stores were torn down to make way for the family's new business venture, the Auburndale Village Shopping Center. When the center was first completed a Kroger Grocery Store, Super X Drug Store, Heitzman's Bakery, a Laundromat, and various small stores were in the main shopping center. A Standard Gas Station and a Liberty National Bank were at the corner of Old Third Street Road and New Cut Road where the original grocery and small strip of shops had been.

Top of the photo is northeast. Auburndale Shopping Center is on the west side of New Cut Road. Auburndale Feed and Lumber Company and the Lillian Smith home are on the east side of New Cut Road. Our Lady of Mount Carmel Catholic Church and School are to the northeast of the Smith home. Photograph is courtesy of Jim Fitzgibbon.

Robert Fitzgibbon's oldest son, Bobby, was also a principle developer of the Auburndale Village Shopping Center. He spent 30 years as the bookkeeper and working the floor at the Auburndale Lumber Company in spite of being born with cerebral palsy. He enjoyed being with people and knew all the customers. When his dad died he took over the business. Mr. Jim Fitzgibbon recalls how his brother Bobby made the business his life and was indeed its "heart and soul".

The shopping center soon expanded to the south with the addition of an O & L Variety Store and a Western Auto Store. Kroger expanded about three different times, taking up more store space. Around 1975 the old Auburndale Lumber Company, located on the other side of New Cut Road, was leased to Moneypenny Hardware Store. They're now located at New Cut Road and Outer Loop. In 1980 Swag Hartel started his well known Swag Shoe Store in the shopping center.

In 1987 Kroger had outgrown the shopping center and needed more room. On the east side of New Cut Road the family house and the old Auburndale Lumber Company (at that time it was Moneypenny Hardware) were torn down. The hill the house had sat on was leveled out and a new Kroger Store was built on the site. Kroger has since expanded again, absorbing the shop space on either side.

The Smith-Fitzgibbon family has left their mark on the area, providing stores to meet the needs of the community and encouraging the growth of the South End of Louisville.

Auburndale Village Shopping Center Brochure photograph is courtesy of Jim Fitzgibbon.

Phelps' Hardware Store

Phelps' Hardware Store on Southside Drive started out as a feed and grain store. If you look at the back of the building you can still see the original building that has been added on to over the years. In 1948 Mr. Wesley "Boots" Siegel and Mr. Robert Fitzgibbon bought the store together. It became Siegel Feed and Hardware Store. They started with the feed store and added on the hardware. When they split the partnership years later Mr. Siegel kept the Siegel Feed and Hardware Store.

Mr. James Fitzgibbon and Mr. Michael Siegel both remember their dads had a "chick give away day" at the Siegel Store. It was an annual spring event for a number of years. If you purchased grain and feed you would receive a dozen baby chicks to raise. It was stopped when the rules and regulations about safety of livestock changed and they could no longer give away live animals.

When asked about his dad, Mr. Michael Siegel recalled how he got the nickname of "Boots". He said his grandmother (Boots' mother), decided to name him Wesley. His grandfather never liked that name and always called him Boots.

Mr. Steve Phelps, who owns and operates it today, purchased the store on Derby Day, 1990. It continues the tradition of serving the community, started by the original feed and grain store.

Photographs of Phelps' Hardware Store, October, 2006, are courtesy of Rosemary McCandless.

Gordon's Corner

It seems like the Speedway Convenience Store was always on the corner of Old Third Street Road and New Cut Road but the very same spot was once occupied by Gordon's Corner. Built around the dawn of the twentieth century Gordon's Corner was a popular saloon in which folks enjoyed passing time. Originally owned by Mr. John B. Gordon; it included a grocery and a dry-goods store in the back. The building was a two story wood frame with a large porch. Gordon's Corner was surrounded by rolling farmland and trees.

During the early years, Gordon's Corner evolved into more of a tavern atmosphere. The patrons consisted mostly of farmers, pulling up in their horse drawn market wagons on route to town or returning to their homes.

As the scene changed, Gordon's Corner always played a part. During the 1930s and 1940s, the Fitzgibbon family owned a giant baseball field across the way, which is now home to St. Nicholas Academy/Our Lady of Mount Carmel. The baseball players became regulars at Gordon's Corner before and after their games. A couple of long time residents of the area recalled that Gordon's Corner was one of the only places in Louisville that you could obtain an alcoholic beverage via curb service.

Photograph of Gordon's Corner, July 1973, is courtesy of Betty Scott.

Sometime in the late forties/early fifties, the area saw its biggest changes. First came the gas stations and everything else followed. The farmers began selling their land to developers to make way for popular subdivisions such as Scottsdale, Iroquois Heights, Merlin Heights, Confederate Acres and Candlelight. The commercial businesses began to boom too. There were restaurants, clothing stores, record stores- just about anything a person could want for was available.

Betty Scott, daughter-in-law of John Gordon worked in the kitchen at Gordon's Corner. She noted that the menu consisted mostly of sandwiches but included fish, fried chicken, French fries, homemade barbeque, burgers and bean soup. She told of a large concrete slab in the parking lot. The area had tables and chairs, a concession building and waitresses to wait the tables. On the weekends, country bands would set up on the concrete pad and perform and folks came from all around to dance. Betty remembers if it rained during the day, they would have to go mop up the concrete slab to get it dry for dancing during the evening.

Top: Betty Scott works the kitchen;
Bottom: Martin Scott tends to the bar;
Both photographs are courtesy of Betty Scott.

Gordon's Corner had a commanding presence at the corner of Old Third Street and New Cut Road. It became a popular drop point for the Courier-Journal. Paper carriers would stand in middle of street in front of Gordon's Corner, shouting out the daily headlines and peddling papers to passers by. The paper carriers, like Gordon's Corner became obsolete. The paper carriers were replaced with the modern day honor system vending boxes. John Gordon's children, Florence Watson, John Gordon, Agnes Gordon-Wiser and James Gordon kept Gordon's Corner operating as a restaurant until 1973. At that time, it was sold to an oil company and became a self-service Exxon gas station.

Original ad from Gordon's Corner courtesy of George Pierson

Escher's Grocery

Since 1982, Pizza Hut has called the corner of New Cut Road and Palatka Road home but prior to Pizza Hut; the same corner was home to Escher's Grocery for 56 years. Escher's called it home in more ways than one as Robert and Lillian Escher, the owners, lived in an apartment above the store.

Robert and Lillian Escher competed with the larger chain stores in the area and created their own market niche by providing high quality cuts of meat at prices lower than the larger, union based chain stores. Robert Escher, an experienced butcher, prepared the meats himself using the knowledge gained from a lifetime in the grocery business.

With traffic worn floors and wooden shelves that reached to the ceiling, stepping into Escher's Grocery was like stepping back in time. But Escher's was more than the corner grocery store, it lended itself as a gathering spot for neighbors to catch up on the latest happenings or share a joke with a friend.

T. P. Escher stands in front of Escher's Grocery circa 1920s;
photograph is courtesy of Bobby Escher.

Escher's was not just a successful neighborhood business; Escher's was a good neighbor. They offered their customers personal charge accounts and free home delivery, often delivering to forty homes a day. In some instances Escher's delivery folks picked up prescriptions and other requests to go along with the grocery delivery. Some customers even left keys for them to put the groceries away when they were not home for the delivery.

It was sad when the Escher's announced they were going to sell the store and retire. Escher's Grocery closed its doors on March 1, 1982, ending a much missed family tradition.

Top: Lillian and Bob Escher Senior standing in front of Escher's Grocery circa 1980-1985; photograph courtesy of Bobby Escher.

Escher's Grocery just after demolition
Photograph is courtesy of Lorretta Walker

Pony Heaven Ranch and Buffalo Farm

Many residents of the area have fond memories of Mr. Gregory's Farm at 7601 Third Street Road. It was like having a zoo in the neighborhood. People would park alongside the road and stand at the fence admiring the animals. Some families would take a family drive from other parts of the county on a Sunday afternoon to come see the animals. Mr. Marion Gregory was known to have had a large variety of animals over the years including, ponies, buffaloes, llamas, ostriches, peacocks, pigeons, mules, horses, goats, geese, a reindeer and long horn cattle.

Mr. Gregory didn't always have this farm. He was in the concrete business and had also operated two different Gulf gasoline stations, first at Second Street and Main Street, and later at Taylor Boulevard and Southern Heights. He and his wife Elizabeth and daughter Betty had a home on Taylor Boulevard near the Gulf station he operated. The house sat on three city lots and Mr. Gregory kept four or five ponies there. In the early 1950s he bought the farm on Third Street Road. He and his family continued to live on Taylor Boulevard, but he drove his ponies down Taylor Boulevard/New Cut Road to their new home. Shortly after purchasing the farm Mr. Gregory bought two buffaloes. He went to Lawton, Oklahoma, to get them at an auction. He named them Buffalo Bill, after Buffalo Bill Cody, and Buffalo Betty, after his daughter. His buffalo herd would eventually grow to six. In 1963, after his wife died, Mr. Gregory had the old farmhouse torn down and a new Bedford stone house constructed. He then began living at the farm.

Photograph of Marion Gregory in front of his Gulf Station on Taylor Boulevard, is courtesy of Ted Zirnheld.

Some of Mr. Gregory's family, Mr. Ted Zirnheld (nephew), and his wife Regina, and Mrs. Ethel Glass (niece), and her husband Jack, shared some of their fond memories of "Uncle Maggie". They weren't sure where the nickname "Uncle Maggie" came from, perhaps from his initials M.A.G. They recalled the peacocks roosting on the roof with their strange cries. The neighbors in the immediate area of the farm also remember the peacock cries. They told how he would buy corn to feed the wild geese. He would go out with the corn and call "Ah geese, ah geese, c'mon geese" and the geese would come to be fed. Even after he had to go to a nursing home, a member of the family would take him to the farm each day so that he could feed his geese. They also remembered his white pigeons that would catch corn on the fly. He had a wild crow he called Charlie. He'd go out and talk to it each day and the crow would answer him back. Uncle Maggie always drove a white Cadillac. At one time he had a little white miniature pony, no bigger than a German Shepherd dog. He was very fond of that little pony and would often take it with him in the Cadillac. It would sit on the floorboard of the back seat. He was known to have gone through the drive thru window of the bank with the pony in back. The family also remembered how the llama would spit in your face. Uncle Maggie would tell you to go pet it and laugh when the llama would spit.

Mr. Gregory loved all his animals but sometimes had a hard time protecting them. Several times he had animals hurt by people. His reindeer was shot by someone with a bow and arrow. As a consequence he discouraged strangers from coming on the property. He did not consider himself a sight seeing attraction, but rather a farm with a collection of animals he dearly loved.

As Mr. Gregory got older he began to lose interest and slowed down. He cut back on the number of animals he kept. When he was 94 he entered a nursing home. By that time all that was left of the animals were the geese and ducks. He was just a few months short of his 100th birthday when he died in 2000.

Today the farm site is now Autumn Trace Condominiums. Everyone in the area still refers to it as the place where the Pony Heaven Ranch and Buffalo Farm used to be. Mr. Gregory was a larger than life character who will live on in the stories and legends of the area. A fitting tribute to the man who so loved his animals.

Iroquois Manor Shopping Center

In the early 1950s construction began on the Iroquois Manor Shopping Center at Third Street and Southland Boulevard. The northern section was the first to be completed. Walgreens Drug Store occupied the north corner with a Kroger Grocery Store on the south corner. S.S. Kresge's Five and Dime was located between Walgreens and Kroger. Smaller shops operated on both the Third Street and Southland Boulevard sides. Southland Barber Shop was one of the first tenants. Mr. Ray Cooper, the current owner of the shop, and Mr. Marshall Morrison, a long time employee, remember the early development of the shopping center and, most fondly, the lunch counter at Kresge's and Martha the manager who served a good lunch.

The southern section of the center and the strip of stores on the western edge of the property were built after the northern section had been completed. The grocery in the western strip has many names. Mr. Cooper and Mr. Morrison remember Colonial Grocery, Piggly Wiggly, Park & Shop, A&P, and Austin's Warehouse Grocery were all there before the current Value Market. The southern section on Third Street had a Western Auto at the back side and a Winn Dixie on the southern corner. The Peppermint Lounge started out in this section. At one time the center boasted three grocery stores. People loved to come and shop for the bargains at all three stores.

Photograph of Iroquois Manor Shopping Center is courtesy of Lynn Acres Baptist Church.

The Kroger Store burned down in the mid 1970s. Long time resident of the area, Brad Wilson remembers seeing the black smoke at his house on Southside Drive. The firewall saved the other stores. All that remained of the store was the cement slab it sat on. Eventually the section was rebuilt, but the Kroger Store did not return. Other stores took its place. Recently the center underwent another transformation when Walgreens moved across the street. CVS took the space and tore down the old store. They then built a new store that is separate from the rest of the center.

The following is a list of some of the stores people remembered being in the center over the years. It is not a complete list.

Dipper Dan Ice Cream   Royal Jewelry
Kiddie Kastle   Fashion Shop
Post Men's Store   Stover's Bakery
O & L Variety Store   Iroquois Bakery
The Cheer Shop (cards and gifts)   Wilson's Florist
Southland Barber Shop   Moon Dry Cleaners

The Iroquois Manor Shopping Center has changed over the years in order to meet the needs of the changing neighborhoods around it.

West is at the top of the photo. Photograph of Iroquois Manor Shopping Center is courtesy of Ray Cooper.

Douglas Park Race Course

Upon approaching the intersection of Kenwood Way and Second Street, most folks would look at the massive brick columns, just north of the former Holy Rosary Academy and never realize that they were once the entrance Douglas Park Race Course. Douglas Park was developed by James Douglas. It opened in 1895 as a trotting track and originally included a grandstand and clubhouse. Later Douglas Park rivaled Churchill Downs as a thriving thoroughbred race horse track. By 1918, Douglas Park merged with Churchill Downs. At this time, Douglas Park ceased to operate as a race track.

The Kentucky Jockey Club took ownership of the Douglas Park premises and used it to exercise and stable the overflow horses from Churchill Downs. The grandstand and clubhouse, no longer in use, fell to disrepair and were eventually razed in 1939. Over the years, Douglas Park barns were plagued by a series of fires. On October 26, 1952, a devastating fire completely destroyed the largest horse barn. Al Stogner, lived nearby at the time of the fire. He recalled waking in the middle of the night to find horses

Photograph of Douglas Park Race Course is courtesy of Greg Kastan.

running wild in the neighborhood. As the stable was engulfed in fire, people had opened the stalls, chasing the horses into the night in an effort to save them. Despite the efforts that were made, sixty-eight horses died in the fire.

In 1954, parcels of land were sold off for the development of residential property, churches and schools. The massive brick columns and fading memories are all that remain of this once legendary race course.

Photograph of the brick columns at Kenwood Way and Second Street, looking west, next to the former Holy Rosary High School, August 2006, is courtesy of Stefanie Buzan.

Thornberry's
Contributed by Diane Hoagland

Joseph "Carroll" Thornberry was a butcher who had a grocery store in Highland Park. When the grocery store was purchased by the city to build the Adair Overpass (now part of the Watterson Expressway) over the railroad tracks, Thornberry moved to another location in Highland Park.

Finally, in 1944, Mr. Thornberry bought property on Third Street near Kingston Avenue (the present location of Thornberry's Delicatessen) and built his grocery, where it remained until 1955. The newly opened Iroquois Manor Shopping Center presented competition. As a result, Thornberry added a restaurant to the back of the grocery in 1953. The restaurant, which fronted on Kingston Avenue, was a big success, employing the entire family- Mr. and Mrs. Thornberry and their five children. From 1953, Carroll Thornberry's wife, Ann Evelyn Hall Thornberry, baked all of the pies (a very popular item) for the family business. When the grocery closed in 1955 the restaurant moved to the front of the building and the back was used as a private dining room.

In 1954, a salesman from Sealtest Dairy told Thornberry that the pies were so good that they could be supplied to other businesses. The salesman asked him if he could try to sell them to some of his route customers. The success of this endeavor resulted in the beginning of a wholesale pie business. But it also necessitated the Thornberry's working seven days a week.

So, in 1958 they closed the restaurant and began selling and delivering only pies from the back of the existing building while renting the front of the building as a Laundromat.

In 1960, a delicatessen was begun in the back of the building. Then, in 1968, when the lease on the laundromat was up, the building was remodeled and the delicatessen was moved to the front with the back of the building being used to prepare the food for sale.

Thornberry's Delicatessen, April 2006; photograph is courtesy of Stefanie Buzan.

On January 1, 1979, Thornberry sold the business to his son, Jimmy and his wife, who ran it until it was sold on January 1, 2004 to owners outside of the family. The Thornberry family operated the business at the site for 61 years and had regular customers from all over the city plus from Bullitt and Oldham Counties in Kentucky and Clark and Floyd Counties in Indiana.

Casey Jones Train Store
Contributed by Diane Hoagland

Electric trains began as a hobby for Fred Gocke, but in 1976, Fred and his wife, Mary Ann, opened the Casey Jones Train Store in the upstairs portion of the Girard's Hardware Store at the corner of Third Street and Kingston Avenue.

After a series of moves, first into a hobby shop on Southside drive and then to Oscar's Hardware on Shelby Street, in 1986, Fred and Mary Ann Gocke settled their business into the store front south of Thornberry's Delicatessen (formerly Wintergerst Pharmacy and Wanda's Wallpaper), where it remains today. It eventually became a family business, involving Fred, his wife Mary Ann and their daughter Carol. Carol came directly to the store after school to open in the late afternoon until Fred arrived after work to take over.

At present day, Casey Jones Train Store is one of just three train stores in the Louisville area. To accommodate train enthusiasts, Mary Ann still opens the store on Wednesday and Saturday afternoons.

Photograph of Casey Jones Trains, April 2006, is courtesy of Stefanie Buzan.

It is interesting to note that Fred Gocke's ties to the Iroquois Neighborhood extend well beyond the inception of Casey Jones Train Store. In May 1947, Fred Gocke's parents, Fred and Veronica Gocke and their neighbors, John and Marge Pfister built the first houses in the vicinity of Third and Esplanade. There were only fields surrounding them on all sides and they had to pay to have sewers extended to their property when the homes were built.

Colonel Walker Flag Company

The Iroquois Neighborhood is the home to Kentucky's largest flag dealer, Colonel Walker Flag Company, located at 313 E. Esplanade Avenue. This unique company has been the proud barer of this title since 1960. As the largest flag dealer in Kentucky, this company reaches out to customers all over the world. Colonel Walker Flag Company was founded by no other than Colonel R. K. Walker himself.

R. K. Walker was born in Louisville's West End. He married his childhood sweetheart, Lorretta in 1948. They moved to Louisville's South End in 1950.

R. K. and Lorretta hosted summer parties on their lawn. It was not uncommon to see John Y. Brown Jr. and Phyllis George Brown, Judge Sternberg and Marlow Cook as well as other well known political figures in attendance. R. K. himself even ran for political office, 6th Ward Alderman and Mayor of Louisville. When R. K. ran for the Alderman seat, the following quote was used in his campaign, *"Everything that I have tried in my life I have been relative successful in. My personality is not one that will let me sit by quietly in the corner and not make waves. If you have a deep, gut feeling that things could be better and you would like a change, then help me. I will give it my best shot!"*

R. K. gets some help from his family during his campaign for Mayor; photographs are courtesy of Lorretta Walker.

In addition to his political background, R. K. had a diverse business background. He owned Magic Melodies Record Company and Schardein Cemetery Inc.; however, for the majority of his career he was involved in the flag business and his family's business, Walker Insurance and Real Estate Inc. The agency had been in his family since it was founded by his father, R. K. "Pat" Walker in 1915. Pat Walker died in 1931 leaving the Colonel's mother to carry on the insurance business until he returned from the service in 1946, following the close of WWII. Although the insurance business prospered over the years, R.K. was always on the lookout for other ways to earn a living.

It was in 1960 that he bought a building and opened a sporting goods store and a stamp and coin shop. Among the many items he sold were the American flag. This proved to be a popular item and he soon stocked more flags and less sporting goods. As for the Stamp and Coin department, burglaries and thefts soon forced a shutdown of this endeavor. With his wife Lorretta managing the Insurance business, R. K. devoted his great energy to building up his flag business. Always a go-getter and active in many civic and veteran organizations, it was not long before the orders for flags began rolling in. In 1985, R. K. suffered a stroke which caused him to have to cut back his activities. He sold the insurance agency and he and Lorretta devoted full time to flags.

For the past nine years, the company has been solely owned by Colonel R. K. Walker's wife, Lorretta Walker. It continues to thrive as a small, family, woman-owned company, operated by Lorretta Walker and her daughters, Donna Walker Mancini and Dana Walker Butz.

Colonel Walker Flag Company prides itself in offering great, friendly service, low prices for the highest quality flags and fast shipment. The company can meet just about any flag or flag accessory need whether it for commercial or residential use. They offer a wide selection of bunting, banners and flag poles along with flags of all varieties; American, state, city, world, military, corporate or special occasion.

A sample of some of the local, famous customers Colonel Walker Flag Company has serviced over the years include; University of Kentucky, City of Louisville, University of Louisville, J. B. Speed Art Museum, Kentucky State Fairgrounds, Baptist East, Actors Theatre, Belle of Louisville, Eastern Kentucky University, Jewish Hospital and Steel Technologies.

The First Doctors

It wasn't until after World War II that doctors began to practice in the area. Up until that time people would have to travel into the city to get medical attention. Mrs. Irma Atwell remembers Dr. Greenfield had a family practice on Evangeline near Southside Drive. She took her children there. Mrs. Edith Hatfield recalls what a kind man Dr. Greenfield was. He was her neighbor on Esplanade.

Doctor John B. Larson Jr. remembers that his father was the first pediatrician in this area. Doctor Larson Sr. was from Iowa and came to Louisville for his residency. He liked it here and decided to stay. Dr. Robert Kidd was his partner and in1948 they opened an office on Woodlawn Avenue. In 1955 they moved to the southeast corner of Third Street and Southland Boulevard. Doctor Larson's family lived on Esplanade Avenue.

Doctor Ed Brockman was one of the first family practitioners in the area. At the end of World War II he was stationed at Naval Ordnance. He liked the area and decided to open a practice at the northeast corner of Third Street and Esplanade Avenue. His son, Doctor Mark Brockman, tells that at the time people tried to talk his father out of opening his medical practice in South Louisville because there were not enough people to make it work. Doctor Brockman opened his practice at the Third Street address with the office downstairs and the family living upstairs. His wife, Marguerite, was his assistant. Many people remember Doctor Brockman's kindness. It was not uncommon for someone to come to his door late at night with an emergency. At the time there were no emergency rooms and the family doctor provided total care. He gave free athletic physicals for DeSales Catholic High School and St. Thomas More Catholic Elementary School. A former coach at St. Thomas More Elementary remembers that if he brought an injured student to Doctor Brockman the student was treated even if he was unable to pay.

Photograph of Dr. Brockman's house and office on Third Street is courtesy of Gloria (Brockman) Montgomery.

Photograph of the Brockman family home at 444 West Kenwood Drive, with the rose garden, is courtesy of Gloria (Brockman) Montgomery.

Doctor Brockman eventually bought the house at 444 West Kenwood Drive for his family. The house was originally built by the Masterson family. The family had several horses and a pony and pony cart. Mrs. Brockman's father and Doctor Brockman built a small barn on the property for the animals. Mrs. Gloria (Brockman) Montgomery remembers growing up in that house and riding horses down Kenwood Drive to Iroquois Park. In later years the grandchildren rode in the pony cart to the park. When the property next door, 500 West Kenwood Drive, was put up for sale the Brockman family purchased it and had more pasture land for the horses. Everyone in the neighborhood admired the beautiful rose garden that Mrs. Brockman's mother planted in front of the house.

Dr. Ed Brockman with Mark and Joe Brockman, (on left), and horses grazing on the front lawn, (on right). Both photographs are courtesy of Gloria (Brockman) Montgomery.

The legacy of Doctors Larson and Brockman continue on in their sons. Dr. John B. Larson Jr. and Dr. Mark Brockman have a pediatric practice at 5109 New Cut Road. Some of their fathers' former patients now bring their children to them.

Parkside Drive-In Restaurant

Parkside Drive-In Restaurant was on New Cut Road, across from Iroquois Park, where the Auto Zone Store currently is. Mr. Jarvis Tramell built it around 1938 and always said that his was the first drive-in restaurant in Louisville. The Tramells lived on Fay Avenue.

Since they were a drive in restaurant, you would park your car and the waitress would come out and take your order. When your order came it was on a tray that attached to your open window and you ate in your car. The restaurant was then known for, and now remembered for, their specials; roast beef on rye or roast beef with mashed potatoes and gravy.

Photograph of Parkside Restaurant, December 11, 1962, is courtesy of Joyce Peck.

Ralph Peck met his wife there when he was working as a car-hop. As Joyce Peck tells it, "I thought he was cute when he came to the car". After they were married Ralph Peck took over the management of the restaurant around May of 1957.

Joyce Peck recalled one time when the restaurant was robbed. A couple of men came in and told the four workers to line up behind the counter. They demanded the money in the cash register. What they didn't know is that while Ralph was standing behind the counter he had been dropping the money on the floor and kicking it under the counter. He saw to it that they took very little money from him that day.

Joyce Peck also recalled how sometimes people riding horses on the bridle path in Iroquois Park would stop across the street and send one person from the group over to buy soft drinks for them. It was a regular stop for some of the riders.

Photograph of the second Parkside Restaurant, March 12, 1963 is courtesy of Joyce Peck.

The old building was torn down in December of 1962 and Ralph Peck constructed a new building on the same site in March of 1963. He continued to manage the restaurant until he retired in 1989. The building was torn down not long after that.

Many people have fond memories of the restaurant, the food and the people who ran it.

Photograph of Ralph Peck in the Parkside Drive-In Restaurant is courtesy of Joyce Peck.

**Kenwood Fire Station
Telesquirt 23 Firehouse**

The Kenwood Fire Station at 706 West Kenwood Drive, (Engine 23), was built in 1956. This was the first year that the area had its own fire station. Engine 23 was first started in

1924, but was located in Beechmont at 501 Ashland Avenue with hook and ladder truck 8. In 1937 the two companies merged to form Quad 8 (an apparatus that has ladders and pumps on it). The other pieces of equipment were used for auxiliary.

Photograph of the Ashland Avenue Fire Station, July 2006, is courtesy of Rosemary McCandless.

On February 1, 1956 Engine Company 23 was reformed and put back in service. It was manned by men from Engine Company 12 and housed in the newly built quarters at 706 West Kenwood Drive in the spring of 1956. The first fire truck of the new station was probably a 1952 Mack pumper. The station has been serving ever since then as the southernmost firehouse in the city of Louisville. In 1992 they became a telesquirt. This apparatus has the ladder and pumper together and an elevated nozzle capable of extending 65 feet. Alan Boucher is the current captain.

Photograph of Engine Co. No. 23, with Captain Alan Boucher and Sergeant Soto-Perez in front of the telesquirt truck, May 2006, is courtesy of Rosemary McCandless.

CHAPTER 8

The Clubs

Kenwood Homemakers ❖ *Kenwood Optimists*
South End Republican Club

Kenwood Homemakers Club

The roots of the beginning of the homemaker's activities in Jefferson County can be traced back to 1918 when Miss Elsie Brunhoff became the first home demonstrator agent for homemakers clubs. Miss Brunhoff held this position from 1918 through 1921. By 1955, a total of 65 homemakers clubs boasted a combined total 1,474 members across Jefferson County. Today, Jefferson County Homemakers continue to keep the tradition of their predecessors alive. There are about 27 homemaker clubs totaling almost 500 members.

The Kenwood Homemakers Club was a group of housewives and young mothers living in the Iroquois area who came together to provide service to the community and share ideas to make each others lives a little more fun and easier. Sally Bush was the first President of the Kenwood Homemakers.

The Kenwood Homemakers; photograph courtesy of Sandy (Bush) Supinger.

A friend of a fellow homemaker said, "You have to remember, there was not much out here at the time the Homemakers Club was in its heyday- these women were teaching each other how to grow hearty vegetables and make soaps and other practical things".

The Homemakers alternated the meeting location from one Homemakers house to the next. Benedictine and pimento cheese sandwiches served with dainty desserts were a common staple at the meetings. The focus of the meetings varied based on the needs of the times. During World War II, the Homemakers and their families banded together to collect scrap metal to aid in war efforts. Other meetings consisted of book discussions or arts and crafts.

Sally, Lovell and Sandy Bush display their scrap metal collection efforts- they collected the most! Photograph is courtesy of Sandy (Bush) Supinger.

Prior to a Homemaker meeting, one of the members would visit the Homemaker's Extension Office to learn a skill or craft. She would return and teach it to the group. Jane Charmolie, daughter of former Homemaker Dot Charmolie, described some of the projects she remembers her mom working on:

♣ 76 RPM records were heated and pulled opposite sides to make a bowl.
♣ Webbing from beneath chairs was embroidered and stitched to make a purse.
♣ Cross stitch samplers, "the hurrier I go the longer I get"
♣ Black metal lunch boxes were lined and decorated to make a purse.

One of the favorite creations of the Kenwood Homemakers Club was the Kentucky Mint Julep Pitcher, made in 1974 to celebrate the 100th running of the Kentucky Derby. The pitcher was designed by the Homemakers under the name "Arrowhill" and produced by Louisville Stoneware. The outside of the pitcher featured instructions for making the perfect Mint Julep. The appropriate measurements were marked on the inside. While supplies lasted, the Homemakers offered the pitcher for $7.95. Each pitcher was accompanied by a small cookbook that included the following message from Homemakers Margarete and Libby:

The gentle, relaxed way of living has all but vanished. The high tension of life today allows little time for just sitting and "sniff, sip and savor-"ing a fragrant drink.

We dedicate The Kentucky Mint Julep Pitcher to those by-gone days. The frenetic cocktail party cannot compare with the simple leisurely enjoyment of a delicious julep shared with good friends.

We hope you will enjoy using this pitcher as a handy reference for making a classic drink, as a container for a bouquet of fresh mint or posies from the garden, as a server for simple syrup, and also as a useful adjunct to your daily cooking as a measuring cup or a mixing bowl.

We are enclosing some party suggestions and a few recipes that we like. They may not be the most typical of Derby parties in Louisville, but they are what visitors have enjoyed at our home and at the homes of friends who have kindly shared their recipes with us.

TRAVELLER'S WARNING: If any guest, after a Kentucky mint julep or two, can not say "sniff, sip and savor," three times, perfectly, don't let him do the driving.

Photographs of the infamous Kenwood Homemaker Mint Julep glass are courtesy of Jane Charmolie.

Kenwood Optimist Club

The Kenwood Optimist Club gave opportunities to children in the South End that they may not have otherwise had. The Kenwood Optimist Club was founded as a branch of Optimist International in 1956. Initially the Kenwood Optimists held their meetings at Hunts Restaurant on Southside Drive. When Hunts closed its doors, the Kenwood Optimists moved to the old Garner's Restaurant at 6821 Strawberry Lane. The meetings were held the first and third Monday of each month at 6:30 p.m. Charlie Otto of Otto Drugs was the Kenwood Optimists first Club President.

The Kenwood Optimists developed a local newsletter simply titled "Info from the Hills". From that, a monthly report was provided to Optimist International. The Optimists kept a handwritten log of each Optimist, their recruits and the year each recruit was inducted into the Club. Each Club President kept an extensive scrapbook, outlining Optimist activities and accomplishments.

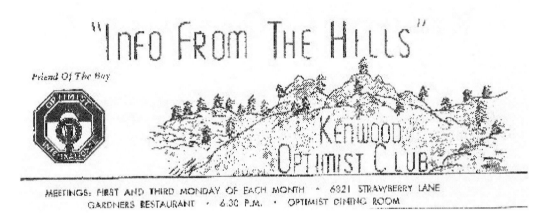

Headline format of the Kenwood Optimist Club newsletter is courtesy of Lorretta Walker.

The Optimists International motto was "Friend of the Boy". The Kenwood Optimists were dedicated to enriching the lives of Children in the South End. They were responsible for fund raisers and educational programs that gave children the opportunity to participate in little league sports and understand the importance of things such as fire safety and prevention program.

The implementation of the fire prevention programs at Louisville Junior Academy, St. Thomas More, Kenwood, Auburndale and Our Lady of Mount Carmel elementary schools was perhaps the most famous accomplishment of the Kenwood Optimists. For many school children, the highlight of the program was receiving their very own fire hat and Junior Fire Marshall Pin; however, the program was so much more than that. The local fire department was onsite to provide fire safety and prevention tips. The children had the opportunity to demonstrate their knowledge of safely exiting the school building in the event of a fire as well as examine the workings of a real fire truck. The first year of the program, Optimist R. K. Walker purchased the fire hats for all of the children.

Children at Auburndale participate in the fire safety program. Notice the traditional fire hats they are wearing. Photograph is courtesy of Lorretta Walker.

The Kenwood Optimist Club was famous for fund raisers. One of the local favorites was the annual Christmas tree lot, located in the parking lot of the old Becker's Florist or the parking lot of the Epiphany United Methodists Church. Former Optimist Bill Buzan has fond memories of working the Optimist Tree Lot; in between customers, he and the fellow Optimists would stay warm around an open fire, eat and catch up with each other. Everyone looked forward to the famous chili made by former Kenwood Optimist President, Al Bosemer.

Kenwood Optimist Club Christmas tree coupon courtesy of Al Bosemer.

In the spring of 1967, the Kenwood Optimists held the "Spring Dance". Committee Chairman, Tom Heslin sent a letter out to fellow Optimists in an effort to boost ticket sales for the dance. The closing of the letter read, *"Come, win a door prize, trip the light fantastic! Feature event of the evening, NO speech by R. K."*

Another activity the Kenwood Optimists were known for was the Annual Charity Flag Day Horse Show held in the outdoor ring of the Kentucky State Fair Grounds. The proceeds were allocated to charities selected by the Kenwood Optimists- the Kidney Foundation largely benefited.

Kenwood Optimist Horse Show at Kentucky Fair and Exposition Center.
Photograph courtesy of Lorretta Walker.

The Kenwood Optimists was widely successful, however, through the years, many of the dedicated Optimists passed away or moved to other parts of town. As a result, over time, the Optimists Club moved from being a part of our community to a part of our history. 2003 was the last year for the Kenwood Optimists Club.

South End Republican Club
Contributed by Beverly Wheatley

Little information has been found on the early days of the South End Republican Club, but documents have been found that indicate its existence in the late 1920s. The purpose of the organization was to support the Republican Party and give support to national, state and local candidates. Events were sponsored by the Club to raise funds and give support to the candidates. No information can be found on the Club after the mid 1930s, but it was, by all indications, active with sizeable membership.

In the early 1950s Justice Marvin and Lillian Sternberg, Marvin and Thelma Stopinski, Bud and Esther Shoo held the leadership positions. Meetings were held the 1st Tuesday of each month at the Beechmont Women's Club on South Sixth Street.

The meetings consisted of a business session and usually a speaker. Most of the monthly programs were civic in nature. There were two meetings a year, one in May and the other in November where the candidates were invited to speak. The May meeting would be quite lengthy because all of the candidates who filed to run in the Primary Election would be invited to the meeting to speak, including the nonpartisan races. The November meeting would feature those candidates on the General Election ballot. These meetings would be heavily attended with standing room only.

Twice a year, usually in October and March, the Club would host a dinner as a fundraiser. In October the ladies of the Club would prepare a turkey dinner with all of the trimmings and it was not unusual to have over 200 people to attend. In March, the fundraiser would be a chili supper. Both of these events were extremely popular, primarily because the cooks were all well known for their good food. The food that was left was sold so people would not only come for dinner but with their containers to take food home with them. Those running for office and office holders would attend these dinners so they could meet and stay in touch with the people. Candidates and office holders would take this opportunity to get workers for their campaigns. So, everyone won, the Club made money and the candidates got their workers.

Photograph of the South End Republican Club is courtesy of Beverly Wheatley.

Photograph of the South End Republican Club in Washington D.C. is courtesy of Beverly Wheatley.

The Club also had a few trips as fundraisers. The trips to Washington D.C. to sightsee and meet with our Congressmen were very successful. These trips took place in the later years of the Club's existence and were discontinued because of the failing health of many of the members.

The Club continued to host an annual Christmas Dinner at Audubon Country Club until 2002. Everyone enjoyed the Christmas Dinner. The ladies did not have to cook. There was always good entertainment and wonderful floral, Christmas decorations donated by Arch Heady that were given as door prizes.

The South End Republican Club is no longer in existence but for over forty years, the Club worked to support the Republican Party, educate its members on the political process and provide social events for the members.

CHAPTER 9

The Elected Officials

Senator Mitch McConnell ❖ *Councilman Dan Johnson*
Alderman David Banks ❖ *The Delahanty Family*
Judge Marvin Sternberg

Elected Officials
Contributed by Fred Banks

The political boundaries have changed frequently over these past 60 years and precinct lines redrawn. A major redistricting was done in the early 1960's following the Supreme Court ruling on "One Man One Vote". The purpose was to have an even population representation in each political district.

Despite these changes, the Iroquois Neighborhood has been mostly included in the 37th and 38th Kentucky State Senatorial and House of Representative Districts, the City of Louisville's 6th and 7th Wards and Jefferson County's "B" District. Commissioners were not elected by District until 1972. Following merger of city-county governments in 2003, our Merto Government representatives are now in the 15th and 21st Council Districts.

The following is a list of elected officials from 1946 to 2006:

Year	Mayor	6th Ward Alderman	7th Ward Alderman	"B" District
1946	Taylor	Bucher	Jones	
1947	Taylor	Ewing	Lattis	
1948-1950	Farnsley	Ewing	Lattis	Lampe
1951-1952	Farnsley	Burt	Lattis	Lampe
1953	Farnsley	Rider	Lattis	Fihe
1954-1957	Broaddus	Rider	Lattis	Fihe
1958-1959	Hoblitzel	Rider	Beckett	Fihe
1960-1961	Hoblitzel	Rider	Lattis	Fihe
1962-1963	Cowger	Buckrop	Korfhage	Fihe
1964-1965	Cowger	Buckrop	Korfhage	Shelton
1966-1967	Schmeid	Buckrop	Wood	Shelton
1968-1969	Schmeid	Kotheimer	Yocum	Archer
1970-1971	Burke	Kotheimer	Lawrence	Archer
1972-1973	Burke	Kotheimer	Lawrence	Kirchdorfer
1974-1975	Sloane	Kotheimer	Lawrence	Kirchdorfer
1976-1977	Sloane	Banks	Lawrence	Kirchdorfer
1978-1979	Stansbury	Banks	Lawrence	Kirchdorfer
1980-1981	Stansbury	Banks	Ross	Malone
1982-1983	Sloane	Banks	Butler	Malone
1984-1985	Sloane	Kleier	Butler	Malone
1986-1988	Abramson	Kleier	Butler	Maze
1989-1991	Abramson	Kleier	Wooden	Maze
1992-1993	Abramson	Johnson	B. Melton	Maze
1994-1995	Abramson	Johnson	B. Melton	Maze
1996-1997	Abramson	Johnson	G. Melton	Maze
1998	Abramson	Johnson	G. Melton	Corradino
1999	Armstrong	Johnson	G. Melton	Davis
2000-2002	Armstrong	Johnson	G. Melton	Delahanty
2003-2006	Abramson	Johnson(District#21)	G. Melton(District#15)	

Year	37th State Senator	38th State Senator	37th State Rep	38th State Rep
1946-1947	Hartman	Shaikun	Coleman	Phillips
1948-1949	McCann	Shaikun	Coleman	Spilman
1950-1955	McCann	Shaikun	Bridgers	Stovall
1956-1957	McCann	Shaikun	Bridgers	Miller
1958-1959	McCann	Young	Burke	Miller
1960-1961	McCann	Young	Osting	Miller
1962-1963	McCann	McGinty	Ballinger	Miller
1964-1967	McCann	McGinty	Bucky	Wright
1968-1969	Beach	McGinty	R. Miller	Wright
1970-1971	Beach	Baker	Kleier	Wright
1972-1973	Yocum	Baker	Kleier	Wright
1974-1975	Yocum	Baker	Kleier	Chandler
1976-1977	Yocum	Baker	Kleier	Wright
1978-1979	Yocum	Meyer	Kleier	Wright
1980-1981	Yocum	Meyer	Paul Clark	Wright
1982-1987	Yocum	Meyer	Paul Clark	Seum
1988-1989	Saunders	Meyer	Paul Clark	Seum
1990-1993	Seum	Meyer	Paul Clark	Butler
1994-1995	Saunders	Meyer	Paul Clark	Butler
1996-1997	Saunders	Seum	Paul Clark	Butler
1998-2004	Saunders	Seum	Perry Clark	Butler
2005	Vacant	Seum	Perry Clark	Butler
2006	Perry Clark	Seum	Weston	Butler

U.S. Senator Mitch McConnell
Responses to questions submitted for Iroquois Neighborhood Book

Where and when did you reside on Kenwood Hill?

We moved to Louisville from Augusta, Georgia, in January 1956 and first lived in a rented house – the last house before Iroquois Park on Southern Parkway. I enrolled at Manual High School as an eighth grader. Then we bought a house at 5509 Westhall Avenue, which was on Kenwood Hill. We lived on Westhall Avenue from the summer of 1956 until sometime in 1963.

When did you play for Beechmont Little League?

During my years there I did indeed play in the Beechmont Little League. I went out in the summer of 1956. That year all of the kids came out and they had a draft. I was pretty good when I was 13 years old; in fact I was the number-one draft pick. I got worse quickly thereafter, but at age 13 I was pretty good. I remember the first team I played on was the Giants, and I know Billy Reed was also on that team. He subsequently became a sports writer for the *Courier-Journal*, and later the *Herald-Leader* and *Sports Illustrated*. The next year I played for the Yankees and Gil Clark, the longtime president of the Beechmont Little League was my manager.

What were your first political experiences?

Some of my first political experiences were in junior high school and high school student council politics. I was vice president of the student council in the ninth grade at Gottschalk Junior High School on Taylor Boulevard. I went back to Manual for the tenth grade and then was elected president of the student body as a junior.

Do you feel that you had any experiences while living in the South End that led you into your very successful political career?

The experience of being president of the student body at Manual High School was a valuable experience because I got to preside over the convocation of students – we had such a big school, the biggest school in the state. In fact, we needed two convocations to accommodate everyone because it was both a junior high school and a high school. So that was a valuable early political experience.

What are your fondest memories of life in our area? Did you spend any time at the Park, or hiking the Hill – Devil's Backbone, etc.? Did you ever spend any time at the Little Loom House, Kenwood Drive-Inn, the Ranch House or the Teen Club?

I remember going to Iroquois Park many times because we lived near the park. I recall playing tennis there and hiking. And I certainly do remember the Kenwood Drive-Inn and the Ranch House. In those days you would pull up to the Ranch House and they put a tray on the side of your car. You placed an order with a microphone and they brought it to your car and you could eat in your car. I also remember going to the Kenwood Drive-Inn. Going to movies at a drive-in theater was a big deal in the 1950s. I also remember the Teen Club at the YMCA on Taylor Boulevard and the dances they held on Friday nights.

I enjoyed living in the South End and I continued to live at home when I went off to UofL in 1960. I didn't live on campus, so I commuted from our home on Westhall Avenue for the first three years of the four years I was at UofL. I have nothing but the fondest memories of that area, and I am pleased that you all are doing a history of Kenwood Hill. I will always remember 5509 Westhall Avenue as a wonderful place of my youth. In fact, I go out there every few years and drive by just to see if the house is being well taken care of.

*Photograph of Senator Mitch McConnell used with permission of
Senator Mitch McConnell.*

Councilman Dan Johnson

Councilman Dan Johnson was elected to serve on the first Louisville/Jefferson Metro Council in November 2002. Previously he served as Sixth Ward Alderman beginning in January 1992.

Throughout his elected service, Councilman Johnson has made economic development and safety issues focal points of his tenure. He led the City of Louisville in its efforts to build a downtown sports arena, and he was an early and strong supporter of merger. In addition, he wrote and led the Board in passing both a gun lock ordinance and an ordinance prohibiting the sale of weapons to minors. And he authored a noise ordinance to control noise pollution and aid in the quality of life in neighborhoods.

Councilman Johnson created and chaired the Drainage Task Force, overseeing drainage issues throughout the city, and he helped initiate the Basement Backflow Program with MSD. He is also a member of the Police Pension Board, Iroquois Neighborhood Association Civic Club, Beechmont Neighborhood Association, Oakdale Neighborhood Association, Pat Greenwell South End Democratic Club, and Beechmont Baptist Church. Councilman Johnson was a member of the Kenwood Optimist Club during the time it was active.

Councilman Johnson is a resident of Kenwood Hill. He likes the many different styles of housing throughout the Iroquois Neighborhoods. He especially enjoys having Iroquois Park and the Amphitheater close by. He is fond of the mature trees that line Southern Parkway and shade the homes in the Iroquois Neighborhoods. He takes pride in the fact that he was responsible for having some of the trees planted.

Councilman Johnson recognizes that Iroquois' cultural diversity is an asset and makes it one of Louisville's most unique places to live. The variety of ethnic restaurants is a real advantage to living in the area.

Councilman Johnson received a Bachelor of Science degree in Political Science Policy Analysis from the University of Louisville. He is married to Sherry Johnson, and has two sons, Andrew and Tommy.

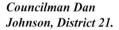

Councilman Dan Johnson, District 21.

Alderman David Banks
Contributed by Fred Banks

David Banks is a 4th generation native of South Louisville. He was elected to the Board of Aldermen for the 6th Ward in 1975 and served as Board President from 1978-1980. This position was the second highest for the city and he was the first South End Alderman to hold that distinction since W. S. Milburn in 1961. His accomplishments include political leadership in improvements to Southern Parkway and zoning restrictions to preserve single family housing, the building of the retaining wall on Kenwood Hill to prevent land slides, the construction of the Gazebo at Southern Parkway and Woodlawn, the preservation of Beechmont Grade School as a Community Center, the Huston Quinn mini park and passage of tough anti-pornography ordinances. After leaving the Board he served as their attorney and played a key role in the Cornerstone 2020 zoning and land use regulations.

He is a graduate of the University of Louisville with majors in Math and Physics and a Juris Doctor. He also has a Master of Divinity degree from Union Theological Seminary in New York and is an ordained Episcopal priest.

David's maternal grandfather was Tom Young, the highly respected Superintendent of Churchill Downs for over 50 years. Tom's love for flowers and landscaping were memorialized by Bill Corum, sports writer and later president of Churchill Downs, in his calling the derby, "The Run for the Roses". Tom's knack for getting the tulips to bloom on Derby Day was widely acclaimed. Together with Earl Ruby, the Courier-Journal Sports Editor and others, he organized the first Derby Parade in 1956. He also built the original Derby Museum in 1962. He lived on Marret Place at the time of his death in 1963.

David's paternal grandfather was Otha Banks, a resident of Beechmont from 1932 until his death in 1955. Otha was Station Master for the L&N Railroad during World War II and Train Master at South Louisville Railroad Yards in the 1950s.

His mother and father, Patty and Fred Banks, are lifelong residents of Beechmont and Kenwood Hill. They have lived on Kenwood Drive since 1976. Patty is active in the Beechmont Women's Club and Fred is a board member of the Iroquois Civic Club/Neighborhood Association. He is retired from General Electric and from City of Louisville where he served as Director of Neighborhoods and Human Services. David's sister, Barbara Banks Sullivan is a Psychology Professor at St. Charles Community College in Missouri.

Photograph of retaining wall erected to protect the homes on Kenwood Hill; taken from South End Campaign News courtesy of Irma Atwell. Pictured are David Banks, Woody Atwell, Glen Brady, Ann Verwys and Fred Banks.

The Delahanty Family
Contributed by Dolores Delahanty

The Delahanty family has maintained an active and strong political and civic presence in the Iroquois area for nearly 50 years. They have lived in the same house on Iroquois Parkway since 1958.

Judge Robert Delahanty served as Judge Pro tem in the Louisville Police Court appointed by Judge Neville Tucker and then by Judge Benjamin Shobe.

When the unified court system was established in Kentucky, Robert Delahanty served on the state wide task force convened by then Chief Justice John Palmore to implement the new court system. As part of the implementation of the court system, Robert Delahanty worked with Ray Weis to implement the Pretrial Release program. Kentucky is one of the few states that eliminated the bail bond system. This radical change in how persons are released pending an arraignment has worked successfully and eliminated many of the abuses of the old bail bond system. In 1978, Robert Delahanty was elected to Jefferson District Court and was elected the first Chief Judge of the Jefferson District by his peers. He remained on the bench until his retirement in 1988.

Photograph of Judge Bob Delahanty, on left, with Judge Martin Johnstone is courtesy of Delores Delahanty.

Dolores Delahanty was a founding member of the National Women's Political Caucus and a co-founder of the Kentucky Women's Political Caucus along with Judge Rebecca Westerfield. The purpose of the organization is to recruit, train and support women who would like to run for political office.

After many years of helping other women run for office, Dolores decided to try to run for public office herself. She ran in the Democratic Primary for Congress in 1994 and lost to Mike Ward. In 2000, she ran for B District Commissioner in the last Fiscal Court before the city and county merger. She won a four year term in a very interesting period during the transition from the old to the new Merged Metro Government.

Judge Kevin Delahanty was first appointed a District Court Judge by Governor Martha Layne Collins in 1986. He was retained as a Judge and has been re-elected since, currently serving on the bench. In 1999, Judge Kevin was elected Chief Judge and served in that capacity until 2001.

Judge Sean Delahanty was elected to Jefferson District Court in 1998 and re-elected in 2002. He is currently on the bench.

Tim Delahanty, a small business owner has always maintained a business in the South End on Woodlawn Avenue.

Shannon Delahanty is Executive Director of the St. Francis Preschool Program and has had a long career in early childhood development.

Terence (TJ) Delahanty received a Master's Degree from Rutgers University. He served in the Peace Corps and was Program Director in Guyana. When he left the Peace Corps, he returned to Kentucky and is now in Youth Development at the University of Kentucky.

Photograph of Judge Sean Delahanty (on left), Delores Delahanty, and Judge Kevin Delahanty, in 1999, the day they were both sworn in, is courtesy of Delores Delahanty.

Marvin Sternberg
Contributed by Joan Sternberg Butler

Born: May 2, 1912
Died: April 28, 1994

Marvin Sternberg was born in Louisville, Kentucky to Manuel and Christina Sternberg who lived on Southern Parkway. He was the third son of four children. His father was Sheriff of Jefferson County during Prohibition, so, Marvin had an early education in law and the justice system.

He graduated from DuPont Manual High School in February 1931, studied law at Jefferson School of Law (now University of Louisville Law School) where he graduated in 1933. He was admitted to the practice of law in 1934.

In 1935, he married a South End girl, Lillian Rafferty, at Bethany Lutheran Church on Southern Parkway. They had two daughters, Tina and Joan.

In 1943, Marvin was appointed Assistant Attorney General for Kentucky and while at this post, took part in ouster proceedings against a sheriff at Covington.

In November 1963, he ran and was elected to the Circuit Bench in Louisville and on July 6, 1964 was sworn in as Judge of the Second Chancery Division. In 1974 Marvin ran and was elected to the State Court of Appeals in Frankfort. This court became the Kentucky Supreme Court in 1975. He served as a distinguished member until January 3, 1983.

Photograph of Lillian and Judge Marvin Sternberg is courtesy of the Sternberg family.

Marvin was always active (as time away in Frankfort allowed) in many civic organizations and was recognized for his tireless service. He was a member of First Lutheran Church, South Park Country Club, Honorable Order of the Kentucky Colonels, Iroquois Civic Club (past President), Kenwood Optimist Club, Masonic Lodge 281, Kosair Shrine Temple, Louisville, Audubon High Twelve Club, the Eastern Star of Kentucky, the Royal Arch Masons # 101, Scottish Rite and Phi Alpha Delta.

Marvin served as Director for the following: Kosair Charities, Jefferson Sportsmen Club, Saints Mary and Elizabeth Hospital and Wettenburg University which presented him with an Honorary Doctorate of Law Degree in 1982.

Marvin received the following awards:
- 1974 Louisville Bar Association Judicial Award for Outstanding Services
- 1975 Distinguished Alumnus Award from Law Alumni University of Louisville Law School
- 1981 Kenwood Optimist Club Respect for Law and Order Award
- 1982 Kentucky Bar Association Award for Exemplary Service
- 1983 Louisville Bar Association Award for Distinguished Judicial Service
- 1987 University of Louisville School of Law, Lawrence Grauman Outstanding Alumnus Award

CHAPTER 10

Did You Know?

Did You Know?

The doctor's offices of Dr. Larson and Dr. Brockman, across from Iroquois Park on New Cut Road, used to be a Burger Chef Restaurant.

Photograph of Standiford Airport, circa the 1960s, is courtesy of Lynn Acres Baptist Church.

The Hollern Chiropractor's office on New Cut Road across from Iroquois Park used to be a Jerry's Restaurant.

At the park entrance at Southern Parkway and New Cut Road there was an ice cream stand that looked like an igloo. There was a giant polar bear beside it.

Grahm's Grocery was at the corner of Shingo Avenue and Lonsdale Avenue.

Elvis Presley's grandparents lived on Beaver Street, off Ashland Boulevard.

The current Walgreens Drug Store on Third Street at Southland Boulevard used to be the site of a Frische's Restaurant.

Girard's Hardware on Third Street used to be Obermeir's Hardware.

Photograph of Girard Hardware, May 2006, is courtesy of Stefanie Buzan.

There was a Wintergerst Drug Store next to Thornberry's. When you got your child's prescription filled Mr. Wintergerst would send a penny bag of candy with the prescription.

The Kaiser Tire Store at the corner of Kenwood Drive and Southside Drive was once Gene Koch's DX Gas Station and later became a Gulf Gas Station.

Rubbies Restaurant on Southside Drive used to be Hunt's Restaurant.

The Rateau children, Henry with Dan (on the sled) and Julian, playing in their yard on Fay Avenue. Photograph, circa the 1920s, is courtesy of Mary Ellen Rateau Clements.

On National Turnpike, right after the railroad tracks, was a large dairy farm owned by the Cook family.

The Family Dollar Store on Southside Drive used to be a Taylor Drug Store. Before that it was an Otto Drug Store and had a soda fountain where you could get cherry cokes (among other things). There was an O and L variety department store next door.

Americana Apartments used to be Lynn Acres Apartments. Mr. Highbaugh, the builder named them for his granddaughter, Lynn.

Photograph of Lynn Acres Apartments, circa the 1960s, is courtesy of Lynn Acres Baptist Church.

Triple Triangle was a fast food restaurant located at Strawberry Lane and Southside Drive, where Tommy's Fruit Stand is currently located.

Behind Colonial Gardens, on New Cut Road was a miniature golf course.

Southside Drive used to be Old Third Street Road until sometime in the early 1950s.

The Ranch House drive-in restaurant included car hops and was famous for Ranch Burgers. It was located at 5225 New Cut Road. This building later became an Ehrler's Dairy Store and is currently the Sao Dem Cafe.

Photograph of William Hendricks with the family's car is courtesy of the Hendricks Family.

At Kenwood Drive and Southside Drive, where Southside Cleaners currently is, was once Paul's Market owned by Mr. Nader.

Smokey Joe's Bar was once at the corner of Southside Drive and Strawberry Lane.

The IGA Pic Pac on Southside Drive used to be a Gateway Grocery.

Auburndale Auto Parts was once the site of Simms Garage, at Southside Drive and National Turnpike.

Photograph of a member of the Simms family crossing Southside Drive near the intersection of National Turnpike, circa the 1930s is courtesy of Margie (Simms) Gibson.

There was a King Freeze at the corner of National Turnpike and Southside Drive, close to where the current Dairy Queen is. King Freeze had square hamburgers like White Castle.

The Callico Club was located where the current White Castle is on National Turnpike.

A large trailer park once sat on Southside Drive (just east of the current rectory of Our Lady of Mount Carmel). There were two streets going south, off Southside Drive, that the trailers were on. At the front of the property there was a shower house since there was no city water in the area. After World War II Mr. Henry L. Pierson and Mr. Chester Lee Grasch bought the property and developed it for homes. Lillian Way was named for Mr. Pierson's mother-in-law and Marytena Drive was named for Mr. Grasch's mother. They built 13 homes on the site.

There was a blacksmith shop, Eyrisch & Grasch, located at the intersection of Southside Drive, (then Old Third Street Road), and National Turnpike, about where the Rite Aid Drug Store is today.

The access road currently used for parking, that parallels Kenwood Drive is where the old trolley tracks were. The trolley turn around was where the Republic Bank currently is.

Photograph of the trolley tracks on Kenwood Drive at Laughlin Avenue, is used with the permission of The University of Louisville Photographic Archives.

There was a trolley line that came up Taylor Boulevard to Iroquois Park. The turn around was just past the Southern Parkway entrance to the park on the east side of New Cut Road.

Photograph of the trolley on New Cut Road/Taylor Boulevard at the Southern Parkway entrance to Iroquois Park is used with the permission of the Filson Historical Society, Louisville, Ky.

Aerial photograph of Simms Garage at the northeast corner of National Turnpike and Old Third Street Road, across from Simms Corner, (current site of Auburndale Auto) is courtesy of Rusty Cummings of Auburndale Auto.

Top Ten List of Thoughts about the Iroquois Park Neighborhood Compiled by Dave Winges

1. Louisville has rich houses, poor houses, dog houses, but only Kenwood Hill can boast of having a goat house.
2. Daniel Boone is said to have carved on a tree trunk in Iroquois Park the phrase, "D. Boone killed a bar." Obviously, he was a hunter and not a speller.
3. A 1905 Sanborn map shows five beer gardens and stands in the Iroquois Park—New Cut Road area. Happily, the location was awash with suds!
4. Stories about Lou Tate's Little Loom House weave a good yarn.
5. In the 1950's the last active horse watering trough was removed from the corner of Marret Place and New Cut Road.
6. An early map of Louisville and Jefferson County show Kenwood Hill as Cox's Knob and Iroquois Hill as Burnt Knob. To this day, these are a pair of the most beautiful knobs in Louisville.
7. A beautiful water curtain with the colored lights graced the front of the stage in the original Iroquois Amphitheatre. However, a sudden gust of wind could dampen the musicians or the audience.
8. Iroquois Gardens, on New Cut Road, south of the Amphitheatre, hosted many notable musical performers. The night Glenn Miller's Band played there in 1941, The Gardens were packed, inside and outside with enthusiastic fans, enthralled by the wonderful music.
9. Iroquois Park had two lookout parking areas. It is doubtful how much "looking out" was done.
10. Fred Senning's Beer Garden, later Colonial Gardens had a small zoo containing a few sleepy animals. Was there a connection between drinking beer and feeding some to the animals?

Photograph of Jacob's Lodge in Iroquois Park, August 2006, is courtesy of Stefanie Buzan.

The following poem won first place in the Courier-Journal's "Where Is Most Beautiful Spot in KY" on August 2, 1925. Author Anna Virginia Mitchell of Louisville, KY received a $15 prize for her contribution.

"Kenwood Hill"

O, beauty is not all in sight
Not all in melody
Nor all in sunny silences
Under a forest tree.
For beauty, is a changing thing.
But here it lingers still
Spreading its magic loveliness
Over a moon-lit hill.

Where every season of the varying year
Brings a new loveliness to greet the eye.
I sought for beauty; and I found it here.
Where slender trees reach up to touch the sky.
I saw it in the wild birds, passing by:
I heard it in the call of the whip-poor-will
And in the thrush's clear unhurried cry.
This is my spot of beauty—Kenwood Hill.

Dogwood in April: bitter-sweet in fall;
In winter, the soft silver hush of snow;
Green leaves in summer; blue sky over all;
Wide spaces where the sweet wild roses grow;
Long cool ravines where narrow streamlets flow
High rocks that be in shadow, cold and still;
Clouds that reflect the sunset's scarlet glow;
These are what beauty gives to Kenwood Hill.

And beauty is not hard to find.
Just half an hour's drive
Down Southern Parkway, until you
At Jacobs Park arrive.
Turn left at Senning's. Just ahead
It will be waiting still.
The fairest State's most lovely spot—
Kentucky's Kenwood Hill.

The Name Kenwood—the Woods of Kentucky
As Believed to be interpreted by Sam Stone Bush

The first syllable of our State's illustrious name "Ken" (tucky) is to be immortalized in a symphony, carrying for all time the very soul and body of virgin forest trees which only God intended should have stood since Sir Walter Raleigh and those "who followed in his trail" first crossed the incomparable "Blue Ridge Mountains of Virginia," and blazed the way to what is now to be enjoyed and utilized as the piece de resistence in the "greater prosperity" of Louisville. It seems justly fitting that our city known throughout the world for its beautiful homes and hospitality, shall point with justifiable pride that this "beauty spot" KENWOOD VILLAGE, has come into its very own, and because of its locality, being at the very door of Iroquois Park, offers no peer in lieu of natural beauty untouched since first our State "gave back the radiance of His smile.

Photograph of Mary Ellen Rateau Clements, Florence Rateau
Thomas and Thelma Crum, circa the early 1940s, on Fay
Avenue is courtesy of Mary Ellen Rateau Clements.

Authors' Note

A great many of the families that established the neighborhoods of Iroquois have been in Louisville for generations. Many of the stories in this book are based on oral histories of their personal remembrances, or stories that were handed down to them from their parents and grandparents. As a result, some of the details or events may differ. We talked to a lot of folks to make this book a reality. If we missed anyone, we would like to take this opportunity to apologize.

Chapter and Cover Photographs

Photograph of the north overlook, Iroquois Park on the front cover is courtesy of The Olmsted Conservancy.

1946 Aerial photograph of Iroquois Park/Kenwood Hill on the inside front cover is courtesy of Daryl Hamrick, James W. Sewall Co.

Photograph of the Little Loomhouse's Esta Cabin, Chapter 1, is courtesy of Lee Ebner.

Photograph of the SS Bush house, Chapter 2, is courtesy of Linda Masterson.

Photograph of vintage Iroquois Park postcard, Chapter 3, is courtesy of Rosemary McCandless.

Photograph of Colonial Gardens, Chapter 4, is courtesy of the Iroquois Branch of the Louisville Public Library.

Photograph of Auburndale School, Chapter 5, is courtesy of Rusty Cummings, Auburndale Auto.

Photograph of St. Mark's Lutheran Church, Chapter 6, is courtesy of St. Mark's Lutheran Church.

Photograph of Simms Corner, Chapter 7, is courtesy of Rusty Cummings, Auburndale Auto.

Photograph of the Kenwood Homemakers Club, Chapter 8, is courtesy of Sandy (Bush) Supinger.

Photograph of the retaining wall on Possum Path, Chapter 9, is courtesy of Irma Atwell.

Photograph of the Trolley car on Kenwood Drive, Chapter 10, is used with the permission of The University of Louisville Photographic Archives.

Photograph of 1926 map of north side of Kenwood Hill, on the inside back cover is courtesy of Linda Masterson.

Photograph of Colonial Gardens on the back cover is courtesy of the Iroquois Branch of the Louisville Public Library.

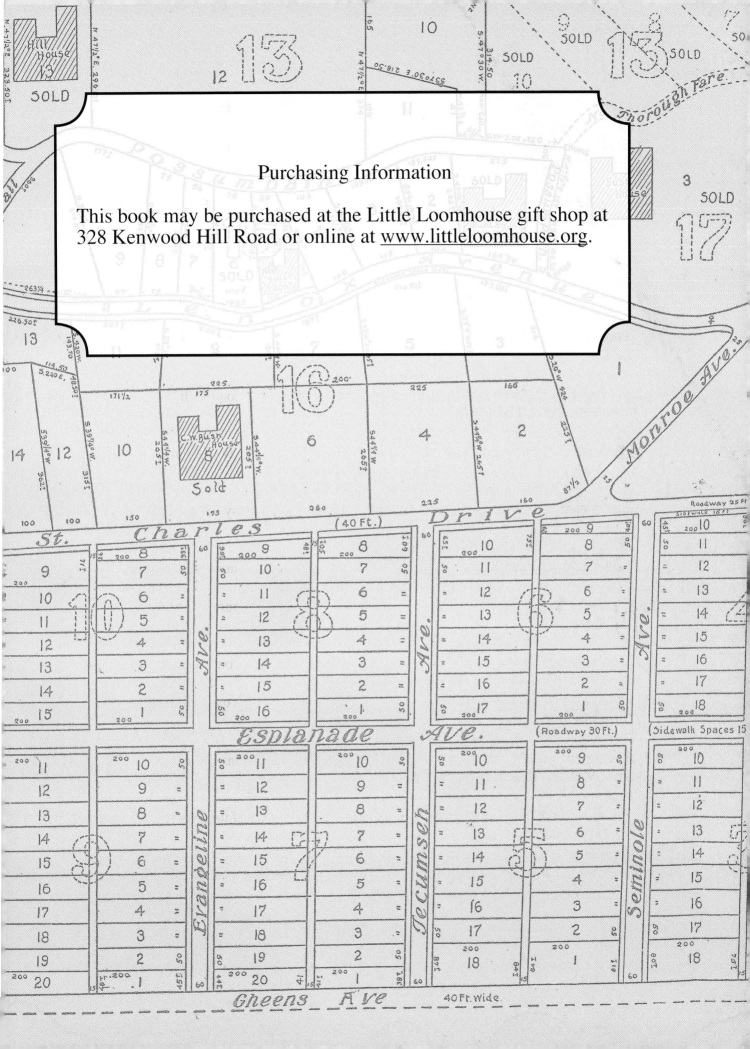

Purchasing Information

This book may be purchased at the Little Loomhouse gift shop at 328 Kenwood Hill Road or online at www.littleloomhouse.org.

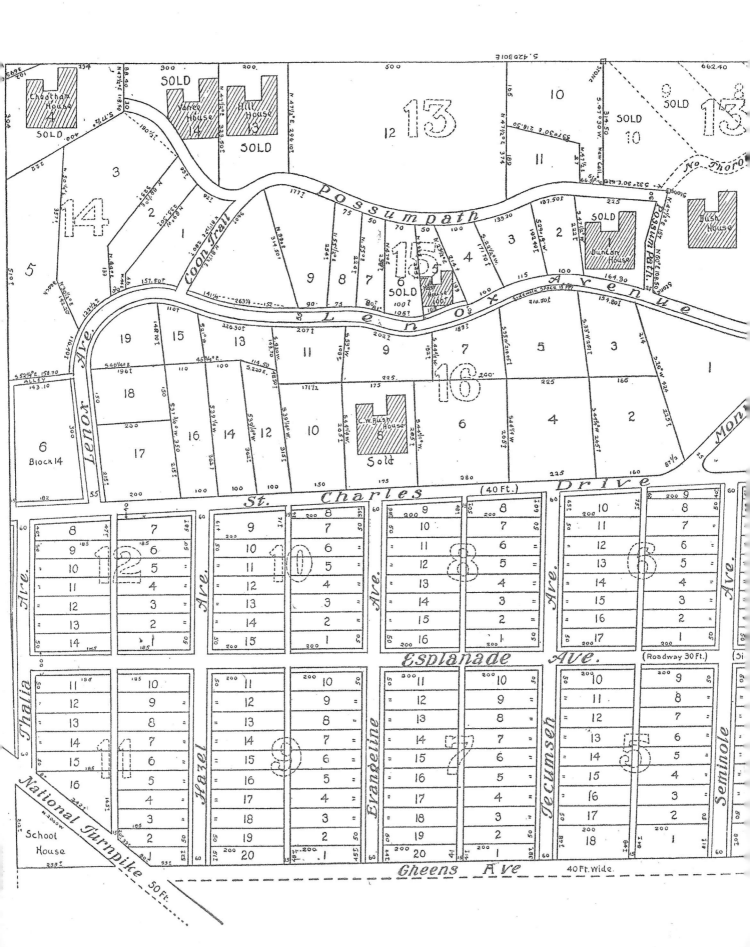